COPING WITH STRESS

About the Author

Dr. Mark Harrold is a Clinical Psychologist who has practised in Ireland for the past 24 years. He writes regularly for *The Irish Times* in the 'Health and Family' supplement and has given workshops in the U.S., U.K., Australia, Romania and Ireland. He is the author of *Parenting and Privilege: Raising Children in an Affluent Society* and regularly appears on radio programmes chatting with Matt Cooper, Miriam O'Callaghan, Pat Kenny, George Hook and Ryan Tubridy, among others. Visit his website at http://drmarkharrold.com.

COPING WITH STRESS

*Techniques and Strategies that
Will Make You Feel Better*

Dr. Mark Harrold

The Liffey Press

Published by
The Liffey Press Ltd
Raheny Shopping Centre, Second Floor
Raheny, Dublin 5, Ireland
www.theliffeypress.com

A catalogue record of this book is
available from the British Library.

ISBN 978-1-908308-96-2

Printed in Spain by GraphyCems.

Contents

Acknowledgements   *vii*

Preface   *ix*

1. Walk   1
2. Breathe   6
3. Talk   10
4. Drink   15
5. Eat   19
6. Plan   25
7. Smell   32
8. Praise   36
9. Problem-solve   40
10. Refuse   49
11. Avoid   53
12. Fail   60
13. Appreciate   65
14. Understand   69
15. Be   75
16. Assert   80
17. Travel   85
18. Sparkle   90
19. Meditate   96
20. Stop   101
21. Listen   106

22. Sleep   111
23. Smile   116
24. Practise   120
25. Exercise   125
26. Pray   130
27. Help   135
28. De-Tech   140
29. Learn   146
30. Write   151
31. Simplify   157
32. Challenge   163
33. Gravitate   169
34. Love   175
35. Colourise   181
36. Habituate   188
37. Garden   193
38. Join   197
39. Do   203
40. Express   208
41. Observe   215
42. Play   220
43. Imagine   225
44. Sing   230
45. Relax   235
46. Move   242
47. Laugh   246
48. Stretch   250
49. Celebrate   254
50. Invest   258

Acknowledgements

I want to thank my wife, Carol, for all her help and support. This project would not have been completed without her. To my children, Patrick and Elizabeth, I have learned more from you than any other source. I am the luckiest Dad in the world. My gratitude extends to everyone I have met on my path to date, even the nasty ones. There was always learning in the encounters. Dr. Jim White, the creator of the marvellous Stress Control programme, has been the inspiration to reach out and help people wherever they are. And finally to David Givens at The Liffey Press, thank you for having faith in my vision.

Introduction

Welcome to my book on coping with stress and thank you for purchasing a copy. It contains my observations on how best to manage stress. They are drawn from both research and real life circumstances. My aim is for this book to be accessible to everyone. I have tried to avoid using psychobabble altogether. Despite all the technological advances made in recent years, stress levels seem to be higher than ever. And the odd thing is that so many people feel alone with their stress. 'Am I the only one who...?' is such a common thought. But most people keep that question to themselves. Always remember that you are not alone in your stress. There are very few people in this world who are not suffering from the effects of stress.

Another question people often ask themselves is, 'Am I going mad?' Be comforted by the fact that if you are asking yourself that question you are most probably not! Indeed, it is a fact that we all need stress to function properly each day. Some experts talk about the inverted U. Essentially, this model suggests that there is an optimal level of stress. Too little stress and we will have difficulty getting motivated. Think of the children of the Celtic Tiger boom who got so much handed to them on a plate. They were never afforded the opportunity to overcome adversity. Too much stress (the rest of us!) and we become paralysed by excessive demands on our time. The optimum is to have the right amount of stress in our lives so that we are at our best most of the time. And that is what this book aims to do.

So the time has come for all the negativity to stop. It is time to take the controls. The objective of the book is to assist you to become your own therapist. There is so much you can do to alleviate stress and it is right there at your fingertips. A good way to use the book would be to treat it as a menu. There are a range of different strategies suggested here and I would encourage you to pick the items that you feel will work for you. So many of us have the best of intentions to do the right things. The ideas are good but the execution is where we fall down.

Perhaps the strongest message from this book is that you must look after yourself first. If you do not do that, it makes the achievement of your goals that much harder. For many of us minding ourselves does not come naturally. It seems to be easier to take care of the needs of others. Make a determined effort to shift focus and put your own needs first. Breach that barrier and look after yourself.

Many of us resort to more self-destructive activities in order to cope with stress. Eating too much of the wrong foods, drinking alcohol excessively and vegetating in front of the TV are all too easy refuges from the pressures of contemporary living. But they provide only temporary relief and make us feel worse in the long run. There are numerous simple alternatives outlined in the chapters which follow. I urge you to embrace these activities. Claim back control of your stress and your life. Live each day like it is your last. The very best of luck.

Dr. Mark Harrold
September 2016

1

Walk

'Walking is man's best medicine'
– Hippocrates (460–370 BC)

So said the father of Western medicine, in Greece all those years ago. Over two millennia on, it is widely accepted that the single best antidote to stress, anxiety or depression remains not tablets, food, coffee or TV, but a good walk. As the famous American wellness guru, Tony Robbins, tells us, we have to move. If we are not moving, our organs will not function as well as they should, our minds will stagnate, our bodies will become ill and ultimately we will die.

The single best way to get moving is to walk. When we are feeling low or stressed, it can be more of a challenge but this is the time when we have to make an extra effort. The hardest part of walking is to get going in the first place, but we rarely ever regret having done it.

Walking is a great way to familiarise yourself with your local area and to engage with nature. When we commune with nature all kinds of wonderful things happen. Remember to take in the smells on your walk, whether it is freshly-cut grass, the bark of a tree or flowers in full bloom. Don't forget to notice the colours which surround you. Becoming aware of the wonders of nature is soothing to the mind and, who knows, they might inspire your next home decoration project. Listen for the sounds of birds or of waves lapping on the shore. And don't forget to stop and observe any animals or birds going through their daily rituals. And, above all, open your lungs and breathe in the fresh air.

The quote below encapsulates the essence of how beneficial a good walk is. I discovered it near a beautiful waterfall in the Blue Ridge Mountains (yes, of Virginia!) while walking there with my family.

> Our minds, as well as our bodies, have need of the out-of-doors. Our spirits, too, need simple things, elemental things, the sun and the wind and the rain, moonlight and starlight, sunrise and mist and mossy forest trails, the perfumes of dawn and the smell of fresh-turned earth, and the ancient music of wind among the trees. – *Edwin Way Teale*

Engaging with nature in this way invariably brings you into the present. We spend far too much time regretting the past and worrying about the future. By embracing these elements on your walk you are taking the pressure off the left half of your brain, which is responsible for gathering information and remembering all the jobs you have to do. Instead, you will be activating your right side, which is responsible for creativity, global thinking and enjoyment. Perhaps this is what Nietzche was talking about when he said, 'All truly great thoughts are conceived while walking.'

In addition, if you are worried about something, a walk can ease the concern. If you are ruminating over a problem, your mind will be clearer after a walk and the solution is more likely to come to you. Or if you simply want a healthy and positive pick-me-up, get your walking shoes on. And by the way, no mobile phones allowed on the walk – this is your time to switch off from daily concerns and appreciate nature!

The benefits of walking are numerous:

◊　It releases happy chemicals into the bloodstream such as endorphins and serotonin.

◊　It burns up chemicals such as cortisol and adrenalin which are caused by stress and which are damaging to the organs of the body when sustained over time.

◊　It doesn't cost anything!

◊　You can do it anywhere.

◊　It is easy on your joints.

◊　It helps to lose weight.

◊　Your mood will be lifted.

◊　Blood pressure is lowered.

◊　Bowel and bladder function are regularised.

◊　Sleep is enhanced.

◊　It slows down the ageing process.

◊　Your immune system is boosted.

◊   It helps prevent heart disease, cancer, type 2 diabetes, osteoporosis and other chronic illnesses.

◊   Your general outlook will be enhanced.

◊   Your creative juices will be triggered.

How much should you do? The general consensus is that 30 minutes walking most days of the week will ensure that you reap the benefits of your efforts. However, you do not have to complete it all at the same time. Two 15 minute walks are just as beneficial. If you can afford it, acquiring a good pair of walking shoes is advisable and would be an excellent investment. Remember to keep an upright gait so you do not miss any of the wonderful sights and sounds around you. It will also help your general posture.

Alone or with others? This comes down purely to your own preference. Personally, I prefer to walk alone. For me, there is nothing more soothing than being alone with my thoughts in the early morning while walking along the coast. Others prefer company so they can talk about the challenges they face or to just let off steam. Still others join a walking club and particularly enjoy the camaraderie of a larger group. Any or all arrangements are good for the body, soul and spirit. What matters is to get started. When we are stressed or feeling overwhelmed, making time and putting in the effort to get walking can be onerous. There are any number of excuses we make for avoiding our walk, such as:

◊   I might meet someone I don't like.

◊   I've too much to do around the house.

◊   It's too cold.

◊   It's too hot.

◊   It's raining.

◊   30 more minutes in bed will do me more good.

◊   I'll have my walk tomorrow.

◊   I'm too tired.

◊   The kids are on holiday.

◊   The dog is having a rest.

◊   My arthritis is acting up.

◊   I have a headache.

◊   My favourite TV programme is on.

Remember, no excuses. As the famous shoe company says, 'Just Do It'. Walking has been proven to be at least as effective as medication for those who encounter stress in their lives. My belief is that it is probably the best therapy of all. So make the effort and plan to go walking, particularly if you are feeling under pressure. You will not regret it.

2

Breathe

*'If you want to conquer the anxiety of life,
live in the moment, live in the breath.'*
– Amit Ray

I cannot over-emphasise the importance of good breathing. As we become immersed in the constant demands of our busy lives, it is unlikely that we notice how this is affecting our breathing. When we are stressed our breathing becomes shallower. Our muscles tense up and our Autonomic Nervous System kicks in. The latter is a response mechanism which becomes more active when we feel stressed. Butterflies in the stomach, palpitations, pins and needles or sweating are common symptoms. The overall effect is that our body goes on alert and the various systems within speed up. Proper breathing can play a huge role in slowing this process down. Breathing is the one element of the Autonomic Nervous System over which we have some control. By learning to breathe properly we can establish a much greater level of control over not just our bodily functions, but our thoughts as well.

How we breathe has an impact on our heart rate, and our heart rate has an impact on our general well-being. High blood pressure is one of the most significant tell-tale signs of stress. And, of course, doctors tell us that elevated blood pressure over an extended period is particularly bad for our health. Indeed, most of us do not use our lungs to even close to their full capacity. If we did, there would be a greater distribution of oxygen throughout the body, which promotes a more efficient general functioning. So there are compelling reasons for focusing on how we breathe.

Did you know that the heart sends about 60 times more messages to the brain than the brain does to the heart? The brain generally sits there waiting to receive messages from the rest of the body. It then responds accordingly by releasing chemicals into the system. So if it receives a message such as an elevated heart rate, it reckons that there must be a threat and releases chemicals that put us on alert. And this happens whether the threat is real or imagined. If the message from the body is that everything is normal and calm, the brain responds by releasing different, feel-good hormones such as oxytocin. Essentially, if you can control your breathing, you can control your thoughts, which, in turn, means you can control your stress.

A simple, but very effective breathing technique goes as follows:

◊ Breathe in through the nose for four seconds.

◊ Hold for four seconds.

◊ Breathe out through the mouth for eight seconds.

◊ Do this three times in a row.

◊ Repeat this sequence at least eight times across each day.

If you stay with this programme you are guaranteed to lower your blood pressure. And, as a reminder to stay with this approach, consider investing in stickers! Buy a sheet of small dot stickers from your local office supplier. Place the dots strategically around your places of work and leisure, for example, on your watch, your computer screen, the car steering wheel, your wallet/purse, or beside the T.V. screen. Every time you see a dot you should stop for about one minute to take the three breaths as described above. I have suggested this simple technique in numerous classes and many participants have enthusiastically described how effective it is. Try it. It works.

Panic attacks are one of the most distressing experiences associated with stress. Hyperventilation, excessive breathing, is at the core of why we have panic attacks. When we are stressed, there is a greater likelihood that we upset the balance of our breathing. Generally, in order to maintain a balance, we inhale oxygen which goes to our lungs and into our bloodstream. There it is converted to carbon dioxide and is eventually exhaled. However, when we breathe in too much oxygen, this delicate balance is upset and the carbon dioxide remains in our bloodstream. The effect is that we can feel unwell or dizzy. It is not these symptoms, though, that cause the panic attack – it is what we say to ourselves about the symptoms, namely:

'I am going to have a heart attack.'

'I am going to lose control.'

'I am about to faint.'

When we learn how to breathe properly, we can minimise and eliminate these symptoms. (For a detailed description of meditative practices which incorporate proper breathing, see the chapter called 'Meditate'.) For the moment, if you are encountering panic attacks, you can regain control of your life by using the simple and efficient breathing technique described above.

The evidence is clear that if we deliberately slow down our breathing, and take deeper breaths by expanding the diaphragm, we will experience a sense of calm and the mind will be more relaxed. Therefore, by changing the way we breathe, we can change our state of mind. It is that important.

Remember:

- ✪ Most of us do not use our lungs even close to their full capacity.

- ✪ Proper breathing will lead to more efficient bodily function.

- ✪ Proper breathing lowers blood pressure.

- ✪ Take the time every day to focus on your breathing.

- ✪ Research a breathing technique that will work for you.

- ✪ Take a class in some meditative practice.

- ✪ Good breathing technique will slow down a racing mind.

- ✪ Proper breathing is a tremendous antidote to stress.

3

Talk

'Talk is not cheap!'

Communication is vital in how we cope with stress. How we talk to ourselves and to others about things that are bothering us is underestimated. Far too many of us keep issues inside which eat away at our confidence, when a better option would be to talk it out. Sharing a problem with others undoubtedly helps to reduce our stress levels. A problem shared truly is a problem halved! And it has been demonstrated that most of what we worry about never happens anyway. There are three types of talking I want to address here.

Firstly, and most importantly, is how we talk to ourselves. Let us take a typical example. You are walking along the street and you see someone you know across the road. As you begin to smile they keep their head down and ignore you. What is your first reaction? Usually, you start to question what you have done to offend the person. This then leads to a conclusion that you are a bad person which further undermines your confidence. You then typically start to question why it is that you cannot keep your friendships going over time. This type of thinking has been labelled 'grasshopper' thinking. We can't seem to help jumping straight into a negative interpretation of even the most minor events.

We have to resist being so hard on ourselves. There could have been any number of reasons why the person ignored you. They may not have seen you. They may have received bad news and didn't want to meet anyone. They may be on their way to the bank to negotiate missed mortgage payments. Most of us are too ready to direct the blame inwardly.

So why do we always seem to conclude that the problem lies with us? This is the type of internal dialogue that we have to challenge and to change. To gain a greater understanding of why this happens, take a look at the picture on the right. What do you see? Do you see the old lady or the young one? If you look at it long enough there are two different interpretations of the same picture. This is exactly what happens when it comes to

our interpretations of the various situations in which we find ourselves. There are always different interpretations. So we should never assume that our initial negative beliefs are the truth. This is particularly because our initial interpretations tend to be negative ones and they are usually directed towards ourselves. They are also usually wrong.

Most often, we tend to be our own biggest critics. We tend to be far too negative in our evaluations of ourselves. There is no better time to change this perspective than *now*. 'I'm too fat', 'I'm stupid', 'I always get it wrong', 'I hate my life' are just some of the common phrases we tend to apply to ourselves. Would we talk like that to anyone we know? Of course not. We are far too ready to be critical of ourselves. This type of self-talk leads to a negative cycle which does, indeed, make us feel worse and undermines our confidence. One of my favourite phrases, which has been attributed to a number of famous people, is, 'Whether you think you can or whether you think you cannot, you are probably right'. Dwell on that phrase for a moment because it is so true in our lives. How we talk to ourselves has a huge bearing on our confidence, our daily functioning and on our ability to achieve our goals.

The next time you find yourself talking in a negative manner, stop yourself and turn it into a positive statement. In general, try to view yourself in a more positive light. Our negative interpretations of ourselves are not what other people see. Like any new approach, adopting a positive dialogue with yourself takes time and practice. You must keep reminding yourself to reinterpret that negative internal dialogue in a more positive way. And this is something which you have absolute control over. Avoid wallowing in self-pity. Of course, we may attribute our negative interpretations to parents who didn't love us enough or because we were bullied at school or work. However, we cannot change the past. We have to leave that behind and live in the present. In doing so, we should aim to be much more kind and understanding of ourselves.

A second type of talk is to talk to friends, family members or your GP. Never allow a concern or a worry to fester in your head. Invariably, you will find that the person you choose to talk to is more than happy to listen, and will help you to find a different perspective on your situation. Having this type of engagement usually brings about a positive result. Problems are rarely as bad as they first appear. Talking it out demonstrates that. If you do not feel better after speaking with a particular person, talk to someone else. Women seem to have less difficulty seeking out the support of friends. Men are more likely to hold their problems inside. I would urge everyone, most particularly men, to talk to trusted friends. It can make all the difference.

A third type of talking is to attend a counsellor/therapist. This can be useful if you are uncomfortable talking to someone you know and prefer to keep your private life separate from your immediate circle. Bear in mind, however, that talk therapy does not suit everyone. There is evidence to suggest that bringing up past history and/or traumas is not the most beneficial course of action if you are feeling out of sorts. Only choose this option if you are comfortable with the format. Talking with someone for 50 minutes once a week will not necessarily bring about the result you might be hoping for. If you do choose this route, make sure you are comfortable with the person providing the counselling. If not, have no hesitation in moving on to a counsellor/therapist who does meet your needs.

Remember:

✪ How we talk to ourselves has a huge influence on how we feel, and on our ability to live positive lives.

✪ Actively stop yourself making negative interpretations, which damage your confidence.

✪ Most of what we worry about never happens.

✪ Practise being positive in your thinking.

✪ Positive interpretations will benefit other aspects of your life.

✪ Always share your problems with someone you trust.

✪ Only choose the counselling route if you are comfortable with that format.

4

Drink

*'Drinking water is like taking a shower on the
inside of your body'*

Since most of our body is made up of fluids, what we drink has a profound effect on how we feel. The good news is that the best drink of all is cheap and plentiful. Water is by a distance the best fluid there is to keep us feeling well. Regrettably, almost equally available are drinks which have the opposite, and even addictive effect. Caffeine-based drinks and alcohol play havoc with the delicate balance we need to feel at our best. In the context of managing our stress, it is important to be aware of both.

If you suffer from headaches, low energy or a general feeling of malaise, there is a good chance that you are dehydrated. While this may seem obvious, it is extraordinary how many people do not drink enough water across the day. By not drinking enough water we are simply unable to function at our best. Despite so many of us suffering the various symptoms associated with dehydration, we rarely make the connection. Consider just some of the benefits of drinking plenty of water:

◊ Boosts the immune system

◊ Assists in optimal brain chemistry

◊ Aids digestion

◊ Assists in distributing oxygen throughout the body

◊ Flushes out toxins

◊ Helps to convert food into oxygen

◊ Boosts energy

◊ Assists in weight loss

◊ Keeps the body in balance

◊ Lubricates the joints

◊ Reduces the risk of kidney stones

◊ Purifies the colon allowing it to absorb nutrients more easily

◊ Contributes to keeping a healthy heart

◊ Clears the skin, making it smooth and glowing.

You are probably aware that the recommended daily intake of water for an adult is about eight glasses per day. And yet, despite this readily available information, far too few of us meet this target on a daily basis. The jury is out on whether caffeine acts as a diuretic or not. Regardless, drinks containing caffeine should not count towards your daily eight. Drink more water and flush out the toxins contained in caffeine-based drinks.

An equally important aspect of what we drink is how it affects our moods. For example, there is plenty of research into the impact of caffeine on the behaviour of children. It impedes their concentration, makes them hyperactive and keeps them awake at night. The negative influence of caffeine is no less for adults. And yet, it is the most consumed legal drug on the planet. Cola is an obvious source of caffeine. Tea and coffee are the other main culprits. Caffeine is a stimulant and it temporarily heightens our mood before our systems plunge back to agitation as soon as the effects wear off. As a result, many people find themselves on an endless rollercoaster of mood swings and jitteriness. This can be very disconcerting, particularly if we are feeling stressed by other issues as well. We end up trying to avoid that dive into moodiness and depression and the headache that goes with it by consuming even more caffeine. And so the endless cycle goes on. Our moods will never stabilise while engaging in this cycle of energy spikes and depletion.

Most of us consume at least one type of caffeinated drink every day. Keep a diary of how many caffeinated drinks you consume. For example, it is extraordinary how few people make the connection between poor sleep and the amount of coffee, tea or cola they drink during the day. Unless you have a very unusual constitution, there is no possibility of having a good night's sleep with significant amounts of caffeine in your system. (There will be more about getting good rest in the chapter on 'Sleep'.)

If you are unable to break the caffeine addiction (and that is most of us), try to substitute some of your daily drinks for healthier options such as herbal or fruit teas, and aim to avoid caffeinated drinks altogether after about 6.00 p.m. As an alternative, a warm milky drink before bedtime will aid sleep.

Many people believe that if they have diet drinks instead of regular ones that they are doing the right thing. Regrettably, one of the main ingredients of most diet drinks is probably even worse for us than caffeine, and that is the sweetener Aspartame. Check the ingredients the next time you are purchasing a diet drink. If it contains Aspartame, put it back! It is considered to be a lethal ingredient by many researchers. Clearly, the advice is to avoid these items altogether. This often comes as a disappointment for those attending my talks on controlling stress. People often feel they are doing the right thing by switching to diet drinks. This is regrettably not the case. The clear message is that to feel well we must drink water – the best diet drink of all.

A final word on alcohol. While this is not a sermon on the evils of alcohol, we need to be aware of its impact on our sense of well-being. We need to know that, as well as being a depressant, alcohol is a diuretic and depletes the body of its much needed fluids. Save yourself those endless trips to the toilet during the night and pounding headaches in the morning by drinking alcohol in moderation (or not at all). If you do consume alcohol, remember to drink plenty of water at the same time.

5

Eat

'Food is essential for life, therefore make it good.'

In order to manage stress it is important that we recognise the connection between our overall well-being and the food we eat. Despite all the information available today on proper nutrition, more processed and junk food is being consumed than ever before. Obesity levels in the developed world are so high that related illnesses such as diabetes and heart disease are at epidemic proportions. Even China, a country whose diet would traditionally have been considered healthy, has developed a notable problem with obesity since the boom in its economy over the past few decades. It appears that the Western diet has infiltrated Chinese culture. And while the physical effects of poor nutrition are easily observed, the psychological problems are not as readily apparent and are more difficult to estimate. What is clear is that the food we consume has a very significant impact on how we function. Poor nutrition contributes to high levels of stress, while eating healthily has a positive impact on our mental health.

There are many sources of information to help us understand the effect of different foods on our health. While diet fads can catch the imagination, it is important to listen to what our bodies are telling us. In his book *Serve to Win*, the great tennis player Novak Djokovic describes how a simple change in diet had a profound impact on his life. From a young age he had a burning ambition to become the best player in the world. He claims that it was the elimination of gluten from his diet that propelled him from being a journeyman professional to becoming the world's undisputed number one player. If a simple change in diet can bring about such a marked improvement in a sport as competitive as professional tennis, what are the implications for the rest of us?

With some very simple changes to our daily routines, striking results can be achieved. For example, low blood sugar can cause poor memory and brain function. Never go for more than three hours without having a healthy snack. This is easy to omit in the bustle of our busy lives. But if we want to be efficient we must incorporate our nutritional needs in our daily routine. Interestingly, many of the most progressive companies in the world are recognising this need and provide areas of rest with free snacks where their employees can rest and renew.

How we eat our food is a further determinant of its impact on our general wellbeing. In order to achieve the optimum benefit from food, avoid eating meals on the run. If you are hungry but don't have time to stop, have a healthy snack and drink some water to keep you going until you have time to sit down and eat your meal in a relaxed way. Eating a meal in tranquil circumstances aids digestion.

There are times when we eat for reasons other than satisfying hunger. Emotional eating occurs when we are feeling sad, lonely or stressed. Indeed, stress produces a hormone called cortisol in the body which causes us to crave fats and sugar. As a result, we make bad food choices, feel guilty and unhealthy, eat more and the cycle of misery goes on. We can break the cycle by being aware of this tendency and looking for another remedy. Step back for a moment and identify the source of the discomfort and problem-solve a solution - perhaps going for a walk, listening to some music or choosing a healthy snack. Keep a food diary in order to identify where and when the problem eating occurs. Aim to replace the bad food with something healthy such as a piece of fruit. Try to eat 'mindfully' which means slowing down the ritual of eating and focus on what you are consuming at that moment. Finally, having noted that stress prompts us to eat unhealthily, we all need a little treat every now and then. So don't be a zealot either!

Given that our dietary choices have such an impact on our psychological health, the focus here is how to optimise our wellbeing with what we eat. Below are some points that you should find useful:

◊ Eat a balanced diet – don't get side-tracked with the latest fad diet.

◊ Eat plenty of fruit, vegetables and herbs to cope with stress.

Eat less CRAP:
C – carbonated drinks
R – refined sugar
A – artificial sweetners & colors
P – processed foods
Eat more FOOD:
F – fruits & veggies
O – organic lean proteins
O – omega 3 fatty acids (fish)
D – drink LOTS of water

◊ Complex carbohydrates (brown rice, pasta, noodles, potato, couscous, muesli, oat-based cereal) have a calming effect and can aid good sleep.

◊ Proteins (eggs, yoghurt, cheese, tuna, beans, chicken, lean meat) enhance motivation and promote clearer thinking.

◊ Fibre-rich carbohydrates (particularly fruits and vegetables) should make up 60-70% of your diet.

◊ Essential fatty acids (EFAs – found in oily fish, sunflower, sesame and pumpkin seeds and real butter) should account for 20-25% of your diet.

◊ Proteins should make up 15-20 % of your daily intake.

◊ Avoid processed foods which, apart from the various chemicals they contain, are often loaded with added fats and sugars.

◊ Eat locally-grown food. It is estimated that foods that are transported across the world lose about 50% of their nutritional value.

◊ Anything that is labelled 'low fat' usually has a high sugar content. Apart from the effect on our waistlines, too much refined sugar fogs the brain.

◊ Have a food allergy test - we can often crave a food to which we are allergic.

◊ Beware the potential adverse reaction to gluten and dairy.

◊ Eat when you are hungry, not when you are feeling sad, lonely or stressed.

◊ Do not eat on the run - if you are hungry but don't have time to stop, have a healthy snack and drink some water to keep you going.

Be aware that certain foods will inevitably cause your mood to fluctuate. There is always an explanation for depressed mood and food plays a big part in that. As a guide, here are some suggestions to set you on your way towards a balanced, healthy and happy food experience.

Good Mood Foods

Oatmeal	Sunflower seeds
Yoghurt	Cottage cheese
Soups	Pineapple
Walnuts	Tofu
Salmon	Spinach
Tea (in moderation)	Bananas
Lentils	Stewed fruits
High protein foods (fish, eggs, chicken, turkey, lean meat)	Whole wheat pasta
Mung beans	Brown rice
Asparagus	Potatoes
Wholemeal bread	Marmite
Orange juice	Avocado

Bad Mood Foods

Chips	Doughnuts
Crisps	Sweets
Pork (ham, rashers, sausages)	Processed foods
Biscuits	Caffeine
Aspartame	

6

Plan

'A goal without a plan is just a wish'

It is rarely just one thing that causes us stress. More typically, a whole lot of issues come at us together and our brain becomes scrambled. Unanticipated bills, work targets, an increasing waistline, parent-teacher meetings, a relationship in decline are just some potential sources of stress. When we are confronted with such issues we invariably do nothing well. And feeling that we are unable to complete tasks efficiently in turn undermines our confidence, which leads to even further stress. It is a negative cycle that many of us are quite familiar with. However, we can change this. By putting structure on our day, our week, our month and our year we establish a measure of control which alleviates stress and actually leads to getting much more done. It does require time to be set aside to plan and make lists. By doing so you will become focused and have a greater feeling of being in control. That sense of being mired in mundane tasks will dissipate.

Steven Covey, author of *7 Habits of Highly Effective People*, gives us a very useful method to create lists and prioritise tasks. There are various versions of his grid. This simple version shows the four different categories of list we should make. Investing time in creating such lists will be time well spent. Because it includes looking after your health, your family and your social life, Section 2 should be given at least equal priority to Section 1. Taking care of yourself and your family is essential to ensure a balanced and satisfying life. So while these aspects of your life may appear on your list as not being urgent, they are every bit as important as work tasks.

There are a few things to keep in mind when creating lists. According to Tony Schwartz, in his excellent book *Be Excellent at Everything*, it is important to be aware of how our bodily rhythms work. He reports from a researcher at McGill University, Debbie Moskowitz, who suggests that Mondays are usually better for completing administrative tasks. This is the day for making those lists! Tuesdays and Wednesdays are our most productive days and we should schedule our most important tasks for these days. This is when our energy is high and our creativity is at its best. By Thursday, our energy begins to drop so the suggestion is to plan activities such as meeting others or undertaking less intellectually challenging tasks on this day. By Friday, energy is at its lowest, which lends itself to more mundane tasks or pleasurable pursuits in which we are more likely to be motivated to participate. The graph below illustrates how, by understanding our natural energy flow across the week, we can operate most efficiently.

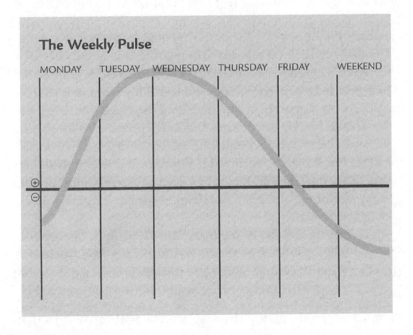

Additionally, the best time of the day to accomplish our goals has been shown to be in the morning. This is when we are at our most lucid. And the recommendation is that we work at a task for no more than 90 minutes. According to Schwartz, the body and mind have a need to rest and renew across the day. For example, he notes that people who are at the top of their chosen professions in areas such as music or computers operate best in time blocks of no more than 90 minutes. Working beyond this time frame means there is a greater likelihood of losing focus. So the objective is to work flat out for 90 minutes with a clearly defined goal to be completed.

Regarding annual goals, or resolutions as they are more typically called, I recommend that you set them up under three headings: Personal (health and self-improvement), Professional (work) and Home (family and household). Review these goals at the end of each month in order to prioritise your shorter-term objectives.

Finally, and with the intention of efficient management of time in mind, a favourite concept of mine is the Pareto Principle. This is also known as the 80/20 rule. Namely, we typically get 80 per cent of results from 20 per cent of our work. Much of the rest of the time is wasted. This is a universal rule that can be applied to a whole range of life circumstances. For example, what percentage of gadgets on your mobile phone do you use? Another version of this rule is that we spend 80 per cent of our time fretting over nasty relatives and only 20 per cent of time with the ones we like. Or we wear only 20 per cent of our clothes 80 per cent of the time. We need to make a determination about how we can make the very best use of our time and plan accordingly. Identify the efficient 20 per cent and expand it. Identify your most efficient use of time and do more of it. Being aware of the Pareto Principle will assist with that.

Remember:

✪ Make time to plan your day, week, month and year.

✪ When setting goals be specific about exactly what you are going to accomplish.

✪ Tuesdays and Wednesdays are the most productive days.

✪ Morning is the most productive time of the day.

✪ Work in 90-minute time blocks for maximum efficiency.

✪ Make time to rest and renew for the best use of time.

✪ Working long hours without balancing family and personal health commitments is a poor use of time.

✪ Use the Pareto Principle to guide you in prioritising your activities.

✪ Complete one task at a time from Sections 1 and 2 (see Steven Covey's grid above) before moving on to the next one.

Below are a couple of simple templates to get you started on planning your goals:

Daily Planner

Time	Action
6:00	
7:00	
8:00	
9:00	
10:00	
11:00	
12:00	
1:00	
2:00	
3:00	
4:00	
5:00	
6:00	
7:00	
8:00	
9:00	
10:00	
11:00	

To do today

Priority	To do list

Notes

Plan

Month: _____   **Year:** _____

Monday	Tuesday	Wednesday	Thursday	Friday	Saturday	Sunday

7

Smell

'The sense of smell can be extraordinarily evocative, bringing back pictures as sharp as photographs of scenes that had left the conscious mind.' – Thalassa Cruso

Of all the senses, the sense of smell is most associated with memory. It is a powerful association and has all sorts of implications for our well-being, both positive and negative. The use of smell can create atmospheres which induce calm or it can bring happiness to a state of sadness. It can awaken our spirits in the morning – having dabbed on our favourite fragrance, we leave home ready to take on the world. Smell can trigger thoughts of beautiful landscapes, specials relationships, journeys to far-flung parts of the world or treasured memories from childhood. Similarly, smells can evoke memories of lost love, tragic events or unpleasant experiences.

I recently went on a trip to London and, while there, I realised I had forgotten to bring my aftershave. Being the vain article that I am, I decided to go and purchase a cheap bottle of fragrance. The only bottle available in the local pharmacy for under ten pounds was Brut. As soon as I splashed it on my face, all sorts of memories came flooding back. There is a whole middle-aged generation from Dublin's Northside who remember going to the Grove disco in Raheny, a rite of passage in the 1970s. Like most of my male contemporaries, I would put half a bottle of Brut on my face in order to assuage my teenage angst. My latter day encounter with Brut reminded me of standing awkwardly in the middle of the dance floor, terrified to ask a girl up to dance. There were only so many times you could go to the toilet during the slow set without people thinking you had a kidney infection, and that certainly wouldn't do! When I eventually got the courage to ask a girl to dance towards the end of the night, she would invariably say 'no', thus ramping up my adolescent awkwardness even further. Of course, after the event I would talk to my mates about the great night at the Grove and all the girls I had chatted up. Oh, the memories! All of this reminiscence came about forty years after the event, and was triggered solely by my application of cheap aftershave in London. That is the power of smell!

Many of us have had that experience of walking through the shops in September and lamenting the presence of Christmas merchandise on the shelves far too soon. One such manifestation is the bags of potpourri scented with cinnamon. One sniff and we are transported, however reluctantly, to the magic of Christmas. Being a foodie, I tend to think of the turkey and ham. Others recall the smell of the pudding, visiting Santa Claus, opening presents. Smell has the power to evoke such strong associations.

With such powerful associations of smells in mind, there is no reason we cannot create pleasant atmospheres in the spaces in which we move on a daily basis. We can conjure calming environments by choosing aromas to match the mood we want to create. There is a whole range of diffusers and scented candles to choose from, easily accessed in the local shops.

In addition, scents can be used to evoke a range of moods, all of which enhance our general sense of wellness. A recent article in the Huffington Post described the power of aromas and the research which has been conducted to demonstrate these benefits. Here are just a few of them:

◊ **Lavender** has a very calming effect and is particularly good for sleep.

◊ **Cinnamon** sharpens the mind and helps us think more clearly.

◊ **Pine** has been proven to alleviate stress (in addition to reminding us about Christmas!)

◊ **Fresh-cut grass** stimulates a sense of joy along with the hay fever!

◊ **Citrus** is associated with being energised.

◊ **Vanilla** has been shown to elevate mood.

◊ **Peppermint** aids concentration.

◊ **Jasmine** has been demonstrated to ease depression.

◊ **Apple** aromas are associated with the easing of migraine.

◊ **Olive oil**, apart from its culinary uses, its aroma has been shown to satisfy one's appetite.

So now that we have established the power and positive influence of smells, the task is to incorporate them into our lives. A few drops of lavender on a pillow will contribute to a more restful night's sleep. Indeed, if you have a child who does not sleep throughout the night, a few drops of lavender may be exactly what is needed. Aromas have an equally positive impact on children. Decide on the type of scent dispenser which best suits your needs and I would suggest that you have one in every room. From a safety perspective, candles need to be watched, which is a slight drawback, given that your primary objective is to create an environment of calm. I would suggest you keep candles for atmospheric dinners and relaxing baths! Pick a pleasing aroma for your car which will keep you alert and create a happy mood. And of course, always dab on a favourite perfume or aftershave to have you in confident mood going out the door each day. Beware of using too much, however, for fear of overpowering those around you! I have to confess to boarding many an aeroplane smelling like a nightclub toilet, having sampled half the aftershaves in the duty free area. Not the most endearing for my fellow passengers! So be warned if you see me boarding the same flight as you in the future!

Decide on the type of ambience you require and choose the essential oil accordingly. The ones mentioned above are simply an introduction to the possibilities. There is a whole range of essential oils with various applications to be found on the Internet. Your local health food shop or pharmacy should also be able to advise you on the most suitable aroma for your needs.

For the moment, don't forget that smells can have a significant impact on how we feel. They contribute to creating environments which help us cope with the pressures of contemporary living and provide the ambience to soothe and renew.

8

Praise

'I can live for two months on a good compliment.'– Mark Twain

What is it about the Irish? We don't seem to have a capacity to give and receive compliments with any level of enthusiasm. Admiration of the work of others seems to be grudging and laden with derision. Could this be a symptom of the daily stresses we encounter or simply a cultural quirk? I believe it is a bit of both. But either way, the absence of a capacity to give and receive praise creates stress. Praise is such a powerful tool for both the giver and the receiver. We have to work on it. My favourite poet, Pat Ingoldsby, encapsulates it perfectly in this poem:

Irish Compliment

'I saw your little television programme
... by accident...
and I have to give you this much...
you're not the worst of them.'
That is as good as it's going to get.

(from *Poems So Fresh and New...Yahoo!*)

There is a tendency to believe that the person already knows we like them or that they do not need recognition as they are confident enough already. Never assume either. We never tire of being complimented. But beware of the backhanded compliment! A friend of mine was told by her sister-in-law, 'Your dress is lovely. You don't look nearly as plump as you normally do'. So it really depends on how the compliment is delivered.

Compliments should be a positive experience for both the giver and for the recipient. There is pleasure in making others feel good about themselves, and who doesn't love to hear something positive about themselves? There are some basic rules about giving compliments so that the person receives it the way you intended and it sounds real:

◊   Make sure you are looking at the person – make eye contact.

◊   Be specific about what it is you are complimenting. 'I love the colour of your top.'

◊   Sincerity cannot be faked. If you don't mean it, don't say it.

◊   Be enthusiastic in your praise.

◊ Give second-hand compliments – 'I heard you got honours in your exam'.

◊ Practise giving compliments. Make a point of praising those around you on a regular basis.

Even harder for many of us is to receive praise. Compliment: 'Your jumper is lovely'. Typical response: 'Sure that old thing is years old and I got it in Penneys'. It is self-destructive to deflect affirmations from those around us. They are rare enough so we might as well make the most of them! We need to learn how to receive them in a way that makes us feel better and the other person feel better for having made the effort to pay the compliment in the first place. By being willing to accept a compliment, our confidence is boosted and we feel better about ourselves. It is time to start believing compliments. So to receive a compliment in a way that will enhance our confidence, the following apply:

◊ Most often, two words are sufficient: 'Thank You'.

◊ Make eye contact and smile when accepting the compliment.

◊ Reciprocate the acknowledgement by praising the person in return.

◊ Practise receiving compliments. Decide beforehand how you will receive a compliment.

The power of praise goes far beyond the simple giving and receiving of compliments. In the days when I used to travel to the far-flung countries of the world, I often treated myself to a bottle of aftershave in the duty free shop. This resulted in my having a collection of about ten different bottles of aftershave at home. I recall one day when I was walking into my office, one of the secretaries said to me, 'Gosh Mark, I really like that aftershave you are wearing!' Which aftershave do you think I wore every day until the bottle was empty? Of course it was that one. The point here is that praise is a powerful way to influence behaviour. We are far more likely to repeat an action for which we have received a compliment.

Parents, managers, coaches, captains of industry, leaders, teachers, doctors and just about anyone who deals with people (so that means all of us) need to learn the power of praise. Not only do we need to learn about it, we need to do it. We do not praise those around us nearly enough. In the coaching manuals, the general recommendation is that we should praise eight times more that we correct a person or a team. I believe this is a universal principle. It is part of the human condition that we are far more likely to repeat a behaviour for which we have received praise. A child will behave better. An employee will work more productively. A student will study harder. And all of us feel better for having been acknowledged for our efforts.

The use of praise is by far the most effective parenting strategy there is. It is the best way to motivate a team whether it is on a field or in a competitive office environment. It is an indisputable fact that the most important aspect of a successful work environment is the way its personnel are valued by the organisation. Numerous studies have demonstrated that, more than pay rises or promotions, validation from superiors is what creates greater staff morale and retention over time. Sick leave is significantly lowered when staff feel valued. And yet I know very few people who feel valued in their place of work.

Coming closer to home, when was the last time you praised your spouse, sibling, parent or friend? If you have not done so in the last 24 hours, you have one hour to do so! Try it. You will change an atmosphere. You will feel better. They will feel better. And, who knows, they may live on it for the next two months.

9

Problem-solve

Problems are nothing but wake-up calls for creativity – Gerhard Gschwandtner

Having studied psychology for five years in Ireland, six years in America (three and a half in Los Angeles, which probably counts as seven given the 'diverse' nature of the population there!), and twenty-six years practising as a psychologist in Ireland, I am now going to reveal the secret of how I earn my living. The six steps in problem-solving outlined below represent the framework I apply to just about every case with which I come into contact. It is a generic framework which can be applied to any problem. And as many of you get used to the idea of becoming your own therapist, this can be the blueprint for deciding a strategy which will best suit your needs or those of someone you may be assisting. No matter what the issue, if you work to the sequence presented here, you will undoubtedly make progress and will most likely solve the problem. There is no doubt that it works if each step if followed.

One of the principal benefits of problem-solving is that it compels you to break issues down into manageable parts. First, you have to decide what problem you are going to work on. By even making the time to take such action you are creating space and an environment of calm reflection. In the midst of feeling overwhelmed by numerous problems, you begin to create order among the chaos. The framework takes you through a step-by-step process that helps you gain perspective and evaluate all the resources you have at your disposal. By creating this space, you are also giving the creative side of your brain a chance to come up with possible solutions. The outcome of problem-solving is a measured, well thought-out plan to tackle the problem at hand.

There are six stages to the problem-solving framework:

1. Define the Problem

'If I had 60 minutes to solve a problem, I'd spend
55 minutes defining it, and 5 minutes resolving it.'
– Albert Einstein

The development of a clear, objective and complete definition of the problem is essential. Most often, stress comes from our perception of a problem but, as we learned from looking at the picture of the old/young lady in the section on 'Talk', our perceptions are not necessarily accurate. We often engage in 'catastrophising' the problem. By taking time to determine the exact nature of the problem, as Einstein advises, we are well on our way to actually sorting it. Statements such as, 'The house is a mess' or 'I feel awful all the time' are too vague. 'The damp in the master bedroom needs fixing' or 'I need to lose two stone' will yield better results. So take the time to properly define the problem you are going to tackle first.

2. Brainstorm Solutions

At this point in the process, you are only limited by your imagination. Lateral thinking can often produce a potentially successful solution. Aim to come up with at least 10 possible solutions. Write each one down, no matter how bizarre it might seem. It might be worth going for a walk before commencing your brainstorming so that you get your creative juices flowing. Nothing should be excluded.

3. Rate the Solutions

Each option should be considered on its merits and rated. The rating should be out of ten, with ten being the best score and one being completely unworkable. Keep in mind that the feasibility of some options may need to be discussed and developed before you decide on a rating.

4. Select the Most Suitable Options

This does not necessarily mean that only one option is selected. It may be preferable to combine two options which you have rated just below the top option. Further consideration may be required at this point in order to decide what steps to take to address the problem.

5. Outline the Plan

There must be a clear plan around who, what, where, when and how. The written plan should not be much more than half a page in length. It should be simple, clearly written (preferably typed) and easily accessible to make sure you stick to it.

6. Set a Date for Review

The review should take place about every two weeks, and the date for review must be taken very seriously. Failure to complete this step is the rock upon which many a problem-solving plan perishes. It is the most important step in the sequence. Any plan set up must be reviewed. It is rare for a successful plan to be the same at its conclusion as it was when starting out. Adjustments are likely to be needed. If the plan is successful, then you continue with it. If it is not successful, decide what needs to change and adjust the plan accordingly. There is as much to be learned from a plan that has not worked as from one that has.

Let's take an example:

1. Define the Problem

You have to attend a job interview. You define the problem thus: 'I'm nervous about a forthcoming job interview and fear I might make a fool of myself.'

2. Brainstorm Solutions

◊ Don't go.

◊ Bring a bottle of water into the room with me.

◊ Take a tablet to calm my nerves.

◊ Practise deep breathing.

◊ Remember that interviewers expect the candidates to be nervous.

◊ Conduct a mock interview with a family member or friend.

◊ Tell the interviewers I get nervous at interviews.

◊ Plan to ask to go to the toilet when it is getting too stressful.

◊ Write down any questions I might have.

◊ Visit the place I am applying for the job before the interview.

3. Rate the Solutions

◊ Don't go (1).

◊ Bring a bottle of water into the room with me (5).

◊ Take a tablet to calm my nerves (3).

◊ Practise deep breathing (9).

◊ Remember that interviewers expect the candidates to be nervous (7).

◊ Conduct a mock interview with a family member or friend (10).

◊ Tell the interviewers you get nervous at interviews (4).

◊ Plan to ask to go to the toilet when it is getting too stressful (2).

◊ Write down any questions I might have (8).

◊ Visit the place I am applying for the job before the interview (9).

4. Select the Most Suitable Options

◊ Practise deep breathing (9).

◊ Conduct a mock interview with a family member or friend (10).

◊ Write down any questions you might have (8).

◊ Visit the place you are applying for the job before the interview (9).

5. Outline the Plan

◊ Practise deep breathing. Every morning and evening I will spend ten minutes doing yoga breathing exercises that I will source from YouTube.

◊ Conduct a mock interview with a family member or friend. I will contact my sister who is an experienced interviewer within the next two days to conduct a mock interview and provide feedback.

◊ Write down any questions I might have the night before.

◊ Visit the place I am applying for the job before the interview. I will contact the HR manager to arrange a visit prior to the day of my interview.

6. Set a Date for Review

Specify the date that you are going to sit down and ask yourself what went well and what went badly. What did you learn from the whole experience? What would you do differently the next time? Write it down. Do not miss out on this crucial step in problem-solving.

On the following pages you'll find your own problem-solving sheet. Use it!

Problem Solving Sheet

1. Define the Problem

2. Brainstorm Solutions

3. Rate the Solutions

4. Select the Most Suitable Options

5. Outline the Plan

6. Set a Date for Review

10

Refuse

'"No" is a complete sentence. It does not require explanation or justification.'

Picture this scenario: You are at your desk and a colleague comes over and says 'We're collecting €20 each for Joanne's new baby'. You are sitting there thinking, 'I have only met Joanne twice. I don't know the girl and I can't afford it even if I did. I have already turned down my daughter's request for a similar amount to buy a top she wanted'. So what is our typical response? 'Oh that's great. Here you are. Hope mother and baby are doing well.' Inside you are boiling but slightly relieved that you have not been judged as a meanie.

But the overriding emotion is that you want to scream. Does this sound familiar?

Another scenario is you are at the supermarket checkout and there are charity bag packers hovering. The last time you let them pack your groceries they broke two eggs and squashed your bread. So what do you do this time? Typically we say, 'Thank you so much', let them squash our groceries and give them €2.00. Or the person beside you at Mass has been sneezing and snuffling with a cold for the entire service. It comes to the sign of peace and they thrust their hand in your direction. You had a debilitating flu virus for ten weeks last year and want to avoid that plague this time around. What do we typically do? Smile, shake hands and say, 'Peace be with you' and hope the virus doesn't spread. Will we ever learn?

Committing to do something you really do not want to do is one of the most stressful events in the course of our challenging daily routines. Over time, if we become the 'go-to' person in our home, with friends or at our place of work, we end up compromising on the most important issues, for example foregoing personal or family activities. This can engender a loss of confidence and a feeling of being overwhelmed. With a little planning, it is possible to take back control of your time and commitments. But you first have to make the determination that this is an important aspect of your interpersonal skills repertoire that needs to be fixed.

My colleague Dr. Owen Fitzpatrick, in his book *Not Enough Hours*, says: 'When we say yes to someone else, we are saying no to ourselves. When we say no to someone else, we are saying yes to ourselves'. The ability to say 'no' is a fundamental skill we must all learn. What most people need to understand is that saying 'yes' when we would prefer to say 'no' is highly stressful.

Useful guidelines on getting this right come from Dr. Manuel Smith's book, *When I Say No I Feel Guilty*. Dr. Smith describes what he calls his 'Assertive Bill of Rights'. He says we all have the right to:

1. Judge our own behaviours, thoughts or emotions and not worry what others think.

2. Offer *no* reasons, justifications or explanations for our actions.

3. Judge whether we are responsible to provide solutions to others' problems.

4. Change our minds.

5. Make mistakes and be responsible for them.

6. Say 'I don't know'.

7. Be independent of the goodwill of others before deciding what we want to do.

8. Be illogical in making decisions.

9. Say 'I don't understand'.

10. Say 'I don't care'.

Some of us may be uncomfortable with these assertive rights but we should all try to get used to them in order to avoid doing something we would prefer not to do. With that in mind, here are my Top Ten Ways to Say No without feelings of guilt or of being put upon:

1. Clarify your priorities. Remember, you are not obliged to be the solution to others' problems.

2. Develop a strategy of kicking for touch when you feel pressurised into making a commitment about which you

are ambivalent. 'That sounds like a lovely idea, but I will have to check my diary and get back to you.'

3. Practise different ways of saying no. 'Sorry, I'm not in a position to help at this time', 'I would love to go, but I have a prior appointment', 'I can't mind your (cat, dog, child) because I am allergic to them', 'I don't carry cash', 'Someone else got in ahead of you', or just plain old 'no'.

4. Recognise that there are many more worthy causes in the world than you can support. Decide what causes are closest to your heart and stick to them.

5. Offer help on your terms. 'Unfortunately, I can't join the committee for the sale of work but I would be delighted to donate a cake'.

6. Remember that saying yes can mean stress, raised blood pressure, loss of family time, fatigue and decreased performance in areas that matter, when you really want to say no. Don't forget that.

7. Have a generic phrase ready for any situation that causes you a dilemma. For example, 'That does not suit me right now, but I will get back to you if anything changes.'

8. Debunk the idea that the world will cave in if you do not agree to a request. Too many of us are too willing to take on the Mother Teresa or Florence Nightingale mantle. None of us is indispensable and we must remind ourselves that the world will still turn if we say no.

9. Remember KISS: Keep It Short and Simple. You do not owe anyone a long-winded explanation in the event that you refuse a request.

10. Transfer ownership of your refusal to something else. 'My budget won't stretch that far', 'I have a prior commitment',

'I have so much on at the moment, I simply cannot help', 'Thank you for considering me, but I am already committed to...'.

So there you are. Go forth with a new-found confidence to say no despite our cultural disposition to please others. Now is the time to prioritise how you will spend your time. This has to include looking after your own needs and easing back on taking care of others. Dispense of the cloak and offload the crucifix! You are not a superhero or a Messiah, comforting as that may seem at times. In the long run, you are not doing yourself or those closest to you any favours. To be at your best, get comfortable with and practise saying *no*.

11

Avoid

'Never wrestle with a pig; both of you get
dirty, and the pig likes it'

There are times during the course of our lives when we need to raise the white flag and decide that we are not going to get involved in a battle this time around. This can take some strategic thinking on your part, but it would be time well spent. You only have a limited amount of emotional and psychological resources available and it is important to decide how to utilise those resources optimally. And that calls for you to decide, not only what you are going to do, but also what you are not going to take on.

Here are some pointers to prevent being dragged down by negative influences. Avoid the following:

Toxic People

You won't have to travel too far to know who I am writing about here. It can be a bully at work, an intrusive in-law, or difficult neighbours. Whoever they are, once you recognise them for what they are, take the necessary steps to make sure that they do not dominate your life. You may not be able to avoid them altogether, but you should aim to diminish their influence on how you live.

News and Negative Media

There is nothing more depressing that sitting down to watch the news and hearing about hundreds of people being blown up in the Middle East, negative financial forecasts that predict further recession or some natural disaster devastating a far-flung country. And yet, so many of us put ourselves through this on a daily basis. There are numerous sources for all this doom and gloom: TV, radio, Internet and mobile phones are just some of them. Cut them off, shut them down! This constant drip-feed of tragedy takes its toll on our morale. Give your mind some space for more positivity and creativity. It does not mean that you don't care about these issues. But nobody has an unlimited amount of compassion and sometimes we need to conserve it for issues which are closer to home and family.

Borderline Personalities

This is the kind of person who sticks to you like glue. You are in a constant cycle of being either their very best friend or their worst enemy. These people have great difficulty in regulating their own emotions, and seem to thrive on screwing up yours! Does this profile sound like someone you know? If so, you need to keep your distance. Borderline personalities can drain the last drop of positivity you have. You will feel constantly under their influence, even when they are not in your presence. Recognise the phenomenon and steer clear!

Nasty Relatives

We didn't pick them but they are there nevertheless. We cannot avoid them completely as there are inevitably situations where they will be present. For example, it has been shown that Christmas Day, which many of us associate with being the happiest day of the year, is in fact the most stressful! It may start out happy enough with the exchange of gifts but can quickly go downhill after some celebratory refreshments, and simmering tensions can suddenly boil over. In general, keep your contacts with nasty relatives formal, limited in time and keep the topic of the conversation general.

Traffic Jams

If there is anything designed to raise stress levels it is sitting in an endless traffic jam when you have an appointment to keep. If you have been practising your meditation routines, then you will probably roll down the window and appreciate the colours in the sky for however long it takes until the traffic moves! For most of us, it doesn't work like that. My best advice is to plan journeys away from rush hours. Travel early if your meeting is at the start of the work day. Take public transport. Cycle if you are fit enough. But stay away from peak traffic situations to preserve your sanity!

Junk Food

We all know what foods we should not eat but very few of us appear to have the capacity to avoid them. Most of us seem to be hard-wired to crave sugar, fat and salt. It is a powerful addiction. The problem is junk food is legal, cheap, there are lots of varieties and it is everywhere. Dr. Donal O'Shea, Ireland's leading expert on obesity, described how one of his patients lost two stone in two months by simply forbidding himself to buy chocolate when getting petrol. There are many insidious means by which marketers compel us to buy these self-destructive products, so we need to be aware of them and develop the habit of healthy snacking instead.

Unnecessary Conflicts

Pick your battles. It is just as assertive to back off from a potential conflict as to take it on. There are many potential crusades we could take on in the course of the day. To keep our stress levels in check, however, we have to choose wisely. Step back from the brink and determine whether it is worthwhile to get involved in a wrangle that is ultimately unlikely to go anywhere good. More often than not, I believe we get involved in rows that we subsequently realise were not worth the effort. That should be the starting point. Ask the question, 'Is this really something I need to dig my heels in about?' Respond accordingly.

An Overly 'Reliant' Friend

Friendship is a great gift. Having someone you can trust and share your concerns with, as well as having fun, is very desirable. It is also beneficial to be able to reciprocate their friendship. But problems may arise when one person's life circumstances change, and there is less time to devote to that friendship. What happens if, for example, you or your friend gets married? If the other person is not capable of changing with the times, he or she may become resentful and stress enters the relationship. This is when you need to define the boundaries if friendship is not to become burdensome.

Comparing Yourself with Others

Very many of us spend a lot of time comparing ourselves with others, and the comparison is rarely a positive one. It is useful to turn things around. Have you ever said to yourself, 'She looks nearly as well as I do?' Many of us seem to be programmed to indulge in self-criticism and in making negative comparisons. If you find yourself doing this, try to turn it around and change the negative internal monologue to give it a positive spin. You are a unique individual and comparisons with others are pointless. Celebrate your uniqueness and don't waste time on envy or self-criticism.

Dwelling in the Past

We cannot access the past, we cannot change it, it's gone. And yet so many of us dwell in the past, regretting actions or blaming distant memories for present unhappiness. While we should all learn from past experiences, it can be extremely upsetting to continually remind yourself of regrets. A far better practice would be to assess what resources you have in the present and make the best of them.

Worrying about the Future

> 'My life has been filled with terrible misfortune; most
> of which never happened' – Michel de Montaigne.

Clearly, most of what we worry about never materialises. Indeed, there is research to suggest that over 95 per cent of what we worry about never happens. So this national pastime (Irish mammies are particularly skilled practitioners) has been proven to be fruitless. Rather than torture ourselves with worry about what might happen, a more fruitful and positive habit would be to plan ahead.

Unrealistic Expectations

Many of us cripple ourselves with unrealistic expectations in various areas of our lives. For example, you are at your weight loss club and the leader announces that someone has lost a stone in a week. This prompts you to expect similar results for yourself the following week. When the spectacular result does not ensue, you console yourself by getting a Chinese takeaway on the way home from the meeting! We have all been there. While we all need to be ambitious for ourselves, we have to temper our aspirations in line with what we can reasonably expect to achieve in order to avoid a sense of disappointment and failure.

Negativity

A positive outlook can make life much more pleasant; however, many of us frequently encounter negativity on a daily basis. Indeed, many people seem to have a preference for wallowing in misery, and they seem to want to drag you down with them. It may be your spouse, your friends, or your work colleagues. Over time, the pessimism can rub off. Develop the habit of switching off when negativity enters the conversation, and try instead to lighten the mood by relating something positive. They will soon get the message that you prefer to hear good news.

Excess

When I lived in Los Angeles, I would bring visitors from Ireland on the obligatory trip to Disneyland. After a while I became tired and bored of 'the happiest place in the world' and it became an irritant. As the saying goes, you can get too much of a good thing! It has been shown that Lottery winners do not become happier as a result of their sizeable windfall. So even too much money can be bad for you! That should be a comfort to most of us!

Drugs (including alcohol and tobacco)

While both can provide fleeting relief from pain or stress, in the long run drugs in all their forms have a major detrimental effect on our well-being. I have buried a number of my old school pals solely as a result of alcohol consumption. Alcohol has been shown to be a depressant that makes us feel a lot worse than we initially did. The evidence regarding tobacco is equally compelling. And the dangers of hard drugs need no explanation. The problem for all of us is the proliferation of all three throughout our communities. Be a role model for your children and avoid them. Children are five times more likely to copy their drug consuming parents in taking up addictive substances.

Recklessness

We have all heard the phrase 'if it sounds too good to be true it probably is'. Always make measured decisions concerning where you invest your time and money. Just think of the thousands of victims of the property boom in Ireland. Despite warnings about the recklessness of property speculation, hearts ruled heads and many poor decisions were made, with disastrous outcomes for so many. Always proceed with caution to avoid unnecessary stresses. Take time before making important decisions.

12

Fail

'Ever tried.
Ever failed.
No matter.
Try again.
Fail again.
Fail better.'
– Samuel Beckett

'You don't learn to walk by following
rules. You learn by doing and falling over.'
– Richard Branson

The fear of failure is more limiting than failure itself. If we are unwilling to overcome adversity then we are going to miss out on most of the richness that life has to offer, no matter where we are. The great American basketball player, Michael Jordan, put it like this: 'I've missed more than 9,000 shots in my career. I've lost almost 300 games; 26 times, I've been trusted to take the game-winning shot and missed. I've failed over and over and over again in my life. And that is why I succeed.' He is widely considered to be one of the greatest sportsmen of all time.

Once we get used to the idea that failure is a good thing, we are well on our way to overcoming many of the challenges we face in our lives. It has been stated that the most successful people in life are the ones who have failed the most. But for us lesser mortals, making that commitment is not so straight-forward. Indeed, for the generation who grew up in the boom years in Ireland, that commitment presents a significant challenge. Far too many of the 'Tiger Cub' generation received their privileges without ever earning them. Their parents made the money and often compensated for their absence by lavishing far too much 'stuff' on them. They are the generation which was never afforded the opportunity to experience and overcome adversity. Indeed, many academics voiced these concerns at the time. They were concerned that 'traditions' such as hard work and delayed gratification were being lost to expectations of media-defined indulgence and one's status being determined by the labels one wore. Studies have shown that, in 95 per cent of cases, wealth does not last to the third generation. The work ethic that created the wealth is spent in the second generation and the third one does not have the tools to sustain it.

The term 'identity dissolution', coined in the US, refers to the problems that can arise if a person is so protected from failure that they never learn how to overcome it. It is detrimental to a person's development to receive everything on a plate, and thus children of wealthy families can face considerable obstacles. If there is no need to strive in order to achieve, the person eventually may see no value in their existence as they have nothing to motivate them. It is traumatic for the person of privilege to realise that there are no challenges ahead and that, if they were confronted with difficulties, they do not have the tools to deal with them.

As parents we need to allow our children to experience failure. This is the only way they will learn how to deal with it – as the song goes, 'pick yourself up, dust yourself off and start all over again!' It is okay for them cry if a race has been lost or if they have not been selected for a given activity. Too often we hand out medals to our children when they have not earned them. Medals should be for the ones who win. The rest need to understand that and make the determination to do better the next time. In making everyone a winner, we are denying children the essential life experience of overcoming a loss. This practice should be curtailed. We have to learn to view failure and the ability to overcome it as a good thing.

Thanks to the Celtic Tiger, for many young people in Ireland material comforts have come so easily that they do not have any insight into the responsibilities and challenges they will face in their adult life. At the same time, those of us from older generations are bemused at the huge differences in lifestyle that have come about since we were at the same stage. For example, where did the 'tradition' of the post-Leaving Cert students' exodus to a Spanish resort for two weeks come from? I believe this absence of opportunity to overcome adversity has left young people at a distinct disadvantage as they negotiate the rest of their lives. It has led to high levels of stress for a whole section of our society. They need to have been given the opportunity to fail and develop their competitiveness by experiencing the cut and thrust of real-life issues. That is what failure does.

A term frequently used in developmental psychology is 'errorless learning'. By taking action, we cannot fail to learn, regardless of whether we win or lose. The greatest challenge is to take action in the first place. After that, we will learn and develop. And there is always something to learn through adversity. This applies to all of us. Working through failure compels us to come up with alternative strategies. It stimulates creativity and teaches us resilience. Failure is an essential life experience and we should embrace it.

Remember:

✪ Failure offers us valuable lessons in life.

✪ Failure teaches us resilience.

✪ There is more learning to be had in failure than in success.

✪ We grow both emotionally and intellectually when we fail.

✪ Resist the temptation to compensate for failures.

✪ Overcoming failure teaches us to ignore the naysayers.

✪ Embrace failure and always ask what has been learned from it.

✪ Allow children to fail as overcoming failure is an essential life task.

✪ The most successful people in life have failed the most.

We all need to understand that failure is an opportunity to learn. We particularly need to teach this to our children. From now on, rather than being stressed by things that go wrong, ask the question: What have I learned from this experience?

A smooth sea never made a skillful sailor
— Franklin D. Roosevelt

13

Appreciate

'Gratitude is one of the most medicinal emotions we can feel. It elevates our moods and fills us with joy' – Sara Avant Stover

'Be thankful for what you have; you will end up having more. If you concentrate on what you don't have, you will never, ever have enough.' – Oprah Winfrey

A golf writer once wrote that he gets up every morning and checks the obituary column in the newspaper. If his name is not there he reckons it is a good day! And that is how it should be for the rest of us. When we get stuck in a negative cycle of stress, there is a tendency to feel sorry for ourselves.

The world seems to be against us. Nothing is going right. We ask ourselves why we are the only ones who have to put up with so much adversity. When we are feeling like this, it is important to take a step back and remind ourselves that, while we may not be able to change the reality of what surrounds us, we can change how we view it. It is our interpretation of what is going on that determines whether it is going to be stressful or not. And no matter how bad we feel about our circumstances at any given time, the fact is that there are many people who are a lot worse off.

There are so many things we take for granted in our life. If we took the time to reflect on and savour these good things, we would be much less likely to feel stressed. Indeed, when we focus on what is going well in our life, it is virtually impossible to feel out of sorts. After my father passed away I found the following poem by Ralph Waldo Emerson in his effects. It encapsulates the message of what should be important for all of us:

What is Success?

> To laugh often and love much;
> To win the respect of intelligent people
> and the affection of children;
> To earn the appreciation of honest critics
> and endure the betrayal of false friends;
> To appreciate beauty;
> To find the best in others;
> To leave the world a little better, whether by
> a healthy child, a garden patch
> or a redeemed social condition;
> To know even one life has breathed
> easier because you have lived;
> This is to have succeeded.

These are the things we should be thankful for. Simple things. That is what matters most. My family never had a car when I was growing up but it was not missed. It is the values my parents instilled in me that have sustained me this far, and I hope they will continue to do so for as long as I live. Never underestimate the enduring value of small gestures and kind deeds between friends and family. A sing-song, a laugh over tea, a handmade card from your child or an apple tart made with love all have tremendous value. We need to recognise and focus on these aspects of life. In doing so, we can minimise and even shut out the negativity which can diminish our life experience. We can only realise our true potential when we seek out and appreciate the positive aspects of our world.

There are so many things to be grateful for in life and one of the things we often take for granted is our health. This is more valuable than any amount of money – just ask a person suffering from a life-threatening illness or a parent raising a disabled child. Another gift we can miss when we are feeling sorry for ourselves is the beauty that is right on our doorstep. Local parks, nearby mountains or lakes, a sunny day, art galleries and libraries are just some of the incredibly beautiful aspects of our environment that we take for granted. Or if you are creaking under the pressures of parenthood (and many of us are), stop for a moment and consider the miracle that is the creation of a child. You cannot put a price on that. And you made that child; a miracle of nature far beyond anything the world of science will ever produce. Another extraordinary gift is the people we meet throughout our life. They enhance our lives as much as we do theirs. These are just some examples of what we can and should be thankful for.

In the humdrum of contemporary living, there can be a tendency to forget all the good things. You may be struggling to see it at the moment, but that goodness and beauty are there. We all have to make the choice to allow ourselves to focus on that. Try to think in terms of the glass being half-full, rather than half-empty. Preoccupation with negative issues drains our energy. Schedule some time for reflection. Seek out all the wonderful aspects of your life, even though you may not feel like it as you read this. Take the time to write down all the positives – there is so much to be thankful for. Decide that from now on your life will be defined by positive sentiment. Do not allow yourself to wallow in self-pity. It is widely acknowledged that being thankful is generally incompatible with stress. By focusing on positives in your life you are taking a giant step towards being in control of your stress. Positivity is a choice. Make that choice. Now.

Remember:

✪ Pause to reflect on what positives exist in your life.

✪ Avoid the tendency to overlook all the good things in your life.

✪ Make yourself focus on the positives and stop dwelling on negatives.

✪ Be thankful daily.

✪ Develop an attitude of gratitude.

✪ Write down two good things that happened to you at the end of each day.

✪ Health is more valuable than money.

✪ Time is more valuable than money.

✪ Use the gifts you have been given.

✪ Pause from time to time and marvel at the wonder that surrounds you.

14

Understand

'Knowledge is the food of the soul' – Plato

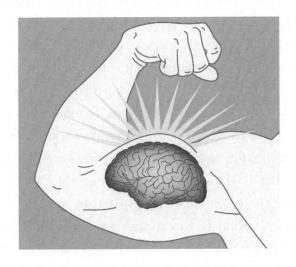

Now for the biology lesson. The human body is a wondrous organism. There are so many complementary systems keeping us going that scientists have yet to fully discover how our bodies work. What is known is that our bodies are constantly working at keeping us well and on an even keel. This is known as 'homeostasis', a term which refers to our capacity to regulate all the complex systems which interact and regulate our functions. When these systems act to protect us, they often produce symptoms we do not understand. When we experience these symptoms and do not know the cause, this can lead to stress.

Before explaining the bodily functions that relate to stress, I want to debunk a common myth. Very often the term 'psychosomatic' is used to describe a person who is inventing symptoms such as headaches or muscle strain and that it is all in their imagination. 'Psych' refers to the mind while 'soma' refers to the body. Rather than suggesting that a person is making it up, this term actually means that the connection between the mind and the body is very real and, indeed, inextricable. This connection is the backdrop to the explanations which follow.

One of our greatest fears is the fear of the unknown. When we do not understand what is happening to our bodies as a reaction to stress, we can become distressed. So begins a cycle where we encounter symptoms, become concerned that something is wrong and become even more stressed by irrational fears that catastrophic consequences are imminent. On the other hand, when we understand exactly what is happening to our bodies on encountering stress, we can rationalise the symptoms. Namely, we can see that there is nothing wrong with us and that our bodies are working perfectly well. In the context of stress, probably the most important bodily response to understand is the Fight/Flight/Freeze phenomenon.

Over many millennia, our distant ancestors evolved a Fight, Flight or Freeze response to protect themselves from the constant threat of wild animals. Upon encountering these threats, the body would automatically go into survival mode. It would challenge the threat (Fight), run away (Flight) or go rigid (Freeze) depending on what the person judged was the best chance of survival in that moment. A raised heart rate to assist running, tense muscles to respond with maximum

strength, loose bowels and bladder to discard any excess in the system, and acute vigilance to observe the threat were just some of the ways this survival instinct expressed itself. These responses were produced by the release of chemicals such as cortisol and adrenalin into the bloodstream. This combination of bodily responses is now called the Sympathetic Nervous System. They were very useful in an era when the threat from wild animals was around every corner. Today, however, they are more of a handicap than a defence mechanism.

Thankfully, nowadays, we are most unlikely to encounter a wild animal when we go down to the shops or play a round of golf! The problem is that we still have this instinct, although, most of the time, we do not need it. The Fight/Flight/Freeze response engages whether a threat is real or imagined. For example, if you feel tense on a crowded train your Fight/Flight/Freeze system can kick in and your brain perceives a sense of threat. It is at this point that your body goes on high alert. However, being stuck on a train, you cannot escape. Palpitations, sweating, feeling faint or nauseous, and hyper-vigilance are just some of the physical manifestations of the Fight/Flight/Freeze response. But you do not need these responses on a crowded train. Your experience in turn can lead you to believe that you are unable to cope and you fear the next such episode. The next time you find yourself in this situation, you may experience additional stress symptoms such as a knot in the stomach or shallow breathing. These symptoms send a further signal to the brain that there is a new threat out there. And so the cycle continues. In a situation like this some people may start to avoid the train altogether. This type of response to stress is very common and very debilitating, so it is important to understand the Fight/Flight/Freeze instinct. While many people start to believe that there is something wrong with them, in fact, these symptoms actually mean that our bodies are working perfectly well – it's just that we don't need to escape from the situation as we are not being attacked by a wild animal.

This mechanism is very much associated with panic attacks, that awful sensation when we feel we are going to lose control. It is far more common than most of us care to admit. When we feel a sense of threat, it is most often this Fight/Flight/Freeze mechanism activating. Most people interpret it as a loss of control. When we have a panic attack various symptoms kick in. For instance, we may start palpitating and convince ourselves that we are going to have a heart attack. How we talk to ourselves in these situations is what leads to the panic attack. The way to break this cycle is to challenge how we talk to ourselves about our stress symptoms. Slowing down our breathing and repeating a calming mantra ('I am in control') will help to alleviate the symptoms. But understanding that the symptoms we are experiencing are very normal reactions to a perceived sense of threat should go some way to making us realise that we are not going mad and we are not going to make a fool of ourselves.

Another aspect of bodily function that is important to understand in the context of controlling our stress is probably best explained by the brilliant Dr. Steve Peters in his book *The Chimp Paradox*. He is the man responsible for coaching numerous world and Olympic champions by teaching them how to manage their emotions, what he calls our 'inner chimp'.

Simply put (and this is a particularly simplified version of the most complex organ in our body), the brain has three main systems. The chimp (limbic system) is the first to receive information from the outside world. It is the reactive and emotional part of the brain and can be hard to control. Dr. Peters suggests that we cannot get rid of the chimp, but we do need to train it. Then there is the 'human' brain which lies in the frontal lobe. This is the logical part of the brain which has the capacity to evaluate what is happening. And finally, there is the 'computer' (the parietal lobe) which stores information. Usually, all three work together. However, there are times when one or another takes over. That is when problems can arise. More specifically, our chimp (the emotional and reactive brain) can often be the first to jump in. It is faster than the human brain and usually reacts before the human brain can engage and make a more reasoned response. Dr. Peters tells us that we have to practise waiting until our human brain engages before responding to any given situation. When we allow the chimp to dominate, there is a far greater chance of the Fight/Flight/Freeze response being triggered, with all the problems that entails.

Remember:

✪ We often react to stress with a Fight/Flight/Freeze response.

✪ While useful when we were living in caves this response is not so useful now.

✪ The bodily symptoms we encounter in stressful situations are part of that Fight/Flight/Freeze response.

✪ People often interpret these symptoms as a loss of control.

✪ Be assured that your body's reaction to stress is normal.

✪ You will not have a heart attack if you experience a panic attack.

✪ You can control these symptoms of Fight/Flight/Freeze.

✪ Practise some of the techniques described in this book to break the negative cycle of thinking.

✪ Aim to slow everything down (i.e. thoughts and actions).

Finally, when we understand what is happening to our bodies during times of stress, we are far less likely to end up in a cycle of distress, which can be potentially devastating. Instead, our understanding allows us to be reassured that our bodily functions are intact and we are not falling apart.

15

Be

'There is no time like the present'

The original, and possibly the best, self-help author, Dale Carnegie, advised us to live in 'day-tight compartments'. In his seminal book *How to Stop Worrying and Start Living*, Mr. Carnegie rightly made the importance of living in the present an absolute priority. Of course, he was not the first to recognise this imperative. Many prominent people, from the great Roman orator Marcus Aurelius to Buddha to American presidents such as George Washington, have emphasised the virtue of living in the present. Interestingly, children have this capacity to live in the present! They have a natural ability to become absorbed in whatever is in front of them. We adults need to take a leaf out of their book. We need to learn how to unburden ourselves of all the issues which seem too easily to build up in our heads and manifest themselves in physical symptoms of stress. The point is encapsulated in the following words:

> Yesterday is history,
> Tomorrow is a mystery,
> Today is a gift,
> That is why we call it the present.

A recent approach to this recommendation of aiming to stay in the present is called mindfulness. You may have heard the term but not understood what it meant. Professor Mark Williams describes it thus: 'Mindfulness is a very simple form of meditation that was little known in the West until recently. A typical meditation consists of focusing your full attention on your breath as it flows in and out of your body. Focusing on each breath in this way allows you to observe your thoughts as they arise in your mind and, little by little, let go of struggling with them'. Mindfulness has been shown to be most effective in treating all kinds of stressful and depressive symptoms. Its virtues have been lauded by people from every walk of life, so it is not just for mystics from the East! Perhaps the best illustration of mindfulness came from a story I heard about a VIP who was visiting a Japanese restaurant. In his honour, he was served the brains of a Japanese blowfish. The rest of this fish is poisonous but the brain is considered a rare and great delicacy. When our celebrity ate the fish he was overwhelmed. The taste, the texture and the delicacy were beyond description. He savoured every mouthful and complimented the chef on his superb cooking. Then a waiter came out from the kitchen very ashen-faced. He apologised profusely and explained that the man had been served the leftovers of his battered cod by accident! It was not the brain of a blowfish after all! This is the essence of mindfulness. Stopping to reflect on the details of what is in front of us takes us away from so much unnecessary worry about events beyond our control.

While it is possible to recognise the merits of this sensible approach to life, it is not so easy to put it into practice. Many of us contemplate past happenings and future prospects in a negative frame of mind. One of the words to describe this phenomenon is 'catastrophising'. We tend to adopt the worst interpretation of situations and assume the worst is going to happen. We have to change this type of thinking.

There are many ways to make ourselves more disciplined in our thinking. One way to address negative thinking is to aim to develop some objectivity to problem situations. Try to step back and ask yourself if you are thinking rationally about the circumstance that is causing you stress. Ask yourself if you are being negative or positive in your interpretation. Check whether you are staying in the present. (The chapter called 'Challenge' goes into greater detail on how to change negative thought patterns.)

Many of the great scholars and philosophers throughout history have taught us about the importance of staying in the present. They can't all be wrong. Make it a priority. Live for now and smell those flowers! Don't forget to read the chapter in this book called 'Breathe'. Breathing slowly and deeply is fundamental to learning to live in the present. Here are some ideas for staying in the present:

1. Eat slowly and mindfully. Notice the texture, flavour and smell of the food you eat.

2. Plan to do nothing for 10 minutes each day. Just sit there and notice what is happening.

3. Use housework as an opportunity to come into the present. There is more to cooking and cleaning than you might previously have imagined!

4. Make a point of noticing things around you. Look out for nice colours, interesting cloud formations or different types of smells.

5. Use a prop to remind you to come into the present. It can be a wristband, a periodic alarm on your mobile phone (you can even get a meditative gong sound) or even a tattoo (if you are into that kind of thing!).

6. Avoid multi-tasking. It is not an efficient way of accomplishing goals and it allows negative thoughts to creep back into your mind.

7. Look at things as if you are seeing them for the very first time. What do you notice?

8. Accept yourself for who you are. Don't compare yourself with others.

9. Surrender to whatever emotion you are experiencing at any given moment.

10. Check in with your senses every so often. What are you feeling, smelling, seeing, tasting or hearing.

11. Play with a puzzle.

12. Play a musical instrument.

Remember:

❂ Live in the present.

❂ We cannot change what has happened in the past.

❂ We cannot predict most of what will happen in the future.

✪ By dwelling on the past and/or worrying about the future we miss the most important bit, what is happening today.

✪ Take time out each day to slow down and come into the present.

✪ Try different techniques for coming into the present and settle on the one that suits you best.

✪ Focus your energy on what is in front of you.

✪ Actively stop yourself getting carried away with unreasonable thoughts. Simply tell yourself to '*stop*'.

16

Assert

*'You have enemies? Good. That means you've
stood up for something, sometime in your life.'*
– Winston Churchill

Have you ever met one of those people who are a bit pushy? They always seem to have an opinion on everything and never listen to yours. Chances are they have been to an assertiveness course! As with everything else in life, we should aim to get the balance right when it comes to engaging with people. Too aggressive and we will make enemies. Too passive and we end up being taken for granted. And, worst of all; passive-aggressive, where we become underhand. 'You got a lovely colour on your holidays. Purple suits you.' Ouch!

Our real aim should be to learn how to assert ourselves so that we can act in a confident way while respecting others. Unfortunately, one of the most stressful aspects of life for many people is the experience of being walked on by others, constantly at the wrong end of even the simplest negotiation. I have heard people complain that they seem to end up buying a round of drinks in a pub far more often than others in their company. Even parents find themselves compromising with their children to the point where the children's demands become totally unreasonable. At work, it is not uncommon for one person to carry the greatest volume of duties while others seem to enjoy a life of leisure. Being constantly used and abused like this takes its toll.

Of course, there are times when we bring this stress on ourselves. Some of us seem to need or want to be a martyr and then protest at being cast in this role. Some of us crave the role of the 'doer' and then resent it when this role establishes itself and you end up being taken advantage of. Once you make the determination that you are going to become more assertive and will no longer be walked upon, the steps to take are clear. Follow the pointers below and see how people will change their reaction to you in a positive way:

◊ Adopt a confident posture. Body language conveys intent. Stand tall and use gestures to get your points across. By behaving in a confident way, the brain responds by producing chemicals that support this feeling of confidence.

◊ Stand up for your right to be treated with respect. Do not accept rudeness and name it if you encounter it.

◊ Ask questions for clarification. This gives you time to respond the way you want to rather than making a snap retort or guilty submission. 'I am unclear what you mean, could you elaborate?' is the type of response required.

◊ Use a firm but pleasant tone of voice.

◊ Avoid perfectionism. Aim to do your best. We often put too much pressure on ourselves to be perfect. If you are having visitors to the house, for example, every room in the house does not need to be hoovered and the windows washed. Take the pressure off and let visitors take you as they find you.

◊ Use the Broken Record technique in order to stay with your point and avoid being dismissed or confused. In other words, keep coming back to your original request or state-ment. For example, you are returning an item to a shop and they refuse to exchange it. Following your request to speak to a manager you are told he is not available. 'I have no doubt he is busy but I won't be leaving until I speak to a manager'. Repeat as needed!

◊ Fogging is a useful technique which involves agreeing with a small aspect of another person's criticism rather than the total assault. For example, if somebody is criti-cising you, tell them that while you accept that your ac-tion may not have met that person's requirement at that time, you have never had complaints of this nature from others. Perhaps the best example of fogging comes from our friend Winston Churchill again when conversing with Lady Astor.

Lady Nancy Astor: 'Winston, if you were my husband, I'd poison your tea.'

Churchill: 'Nancy, if I were your husband, I'd drink it.'

◊ Divert. If you encounter a situation which makes you feel uncomfortable, don't feel you have to deal with it immediately. For example, if you are on the receiving end of an unexpected verbal assault, inform the person that they appear be angry at present and that you would prefer to discuss the topic when you are both calm.

◊ Ask for help. Far too many of us fall down on this particular aspect. And the reality is that people are usually only too willing to provide assistance.

◊ Aim for a win-win outcome from every situation. According to Winston Churchill, 'Diplomacy is the art of telling people to go to hell in such a way that they ask for directions'. This is not the easiest skill but a good starting point is to have a compromise position before starting the encounter.

◊ Say 'Yes' to what you want. This could probably be called the Mrs. Doyle phenomenon. 'Will you have a cup of tea?' In Ireland, we seem to think it is polite to refuse at first in the expectation that we will be offered the item at least twice more. 'You will, you will, you will.' This dialogue is played out time and again in every Irish household. And it can get tiresome. If you are in America don't politely refuse, expecting that you will be offered the beverage again – you will be left watching the person drink in front of you while your thirst remains unquenched! Learn to say 'Yes' the first time. It's okay to do so!

◊ Be decisive. Whatever decision or response you choose to make in any given situation, own it. Get used to the idea of clearly stating your position and following through. You will feel better and so will the person with whom you are dealing. Lack of clarity gets up people's noses and can make you appear weak.

◊ Take a chance. The worst thing that can happen is that matters may not work out exactly as you wanted. But you will enjoy the experience. Life gets so much more interesting when we are willing to push the boundaries.

◊ Question authority! Just because a person's status gives them a position of power does not mean they are right. What a pity the voices of reason were not heeded before our whole nation was plunged into debt for a generation or more. Don't be afraid to seek full information when dealing with professionals, such as meeting with your doctor. Write down your questions beforehand to ensure all your concerns are covered.

Asserting our fundamental rights alleviates much of our stress. There are other chapters in the book which will add to your assertiveness repertoire. Remember, being assertive does not mean becoming aggressive. As with most aspects of managing stress, our task is to work on getting the balance right. Have fun in finding that place.

17

Travel

*'Travel is the only thing you buy, that makes
you richer'*

I have never regretted a penny I have spent on travel. And there have been quite a few of them spent! There are so many benefits to taking a break from our usual routines. One of the most striking aspects of travel is how similar human nature is the world over. Most people are friendly and kind and most people want to live happy and secure lives, free of the badness of the few. And you learn that a smile is universal.

So how can the benefits of travel be encapsulated in a few brief words? Daranna Gidel is quoted as saying: 'Sometimes you lose sight of things ... and when you travel everything balances out.' An even simpler quote comes from David Mitchell, 'Travel far enough, you meet yourself'. Even recent research on creating the optimal work environment emphasises the importance of regular breaks away from the humdrum of the workplace. Indeed, many of the most successful companies insist on their valued employees taking extended sabbatical breaks periodically so that they come back renewed and full of vigour. As a committed globetrotter in the years before children came on the scene, the various encounters I enjoyed could never be encapsulated in a book on stress. But here are just some of the broadening experiences travel has gifted me.

When planning my trip through China, I decided to bring chocolate sweets in the event that I visited a school. Our tour party had occasion to visit a rural village in central China and this seemed the perfect time to offload my prized Western gift. The children were following our tour party around like we were a collective of Pied Pipers. They took the sweets enthusiastically but, to a child, they all instantly spat them out. Quickly they moved on to the lady who was distributing pencils. They were far more interested in an educational tool than in Western junk food that they had never tasted.

While leaving Dublin airport to travel to Russia I remembered a guidebook had said that ladies tights were a prized item there and were useful exchange items. I asked my sister to buy some in the shop as I was too embarrassed to buy them myself. Armed with my precious commodity, I confidently strode through the tourist market in Moscow assuming I could pick anything in exchange for the tights. I selected an elaborate collection of about 15 hand-painted matrioshka dolls (the ones that fit inside each other) and asked the seller if he did exchanges. He asked me to show him what I had in return. When I told him that I had three pairs of ladies tights, he started laughing out loud and picked up a tiny little single doll and said he would give me that. It was one of the most embarrassing moments of my life! How could I have ended up on a street in Moscow offering ladies tights to a street vendor, I wondered, my face the colour of a ripe tomato. Clearly, Russia had moved on. I had not. That guidebook went in the bin.

Closer to home, I had occasion to travel to Kerry with my family a few years ago. We met up with a distant relative who had buried her husband a few months earlier. I had not seen her since her loss. My instant response upon meeting was to lean over, lips puckered to plant a big kiss on her cheek and give her a bear hug. She stiffened up and reacted like she had been attacked by a dribbling St. Bernard dog. Having delivered my greeting, I pulled back and we were both embarrassed. I learned then that many people in rural Ireland are more formal in their greetings, whether the occasion is happy or sad. The next time we met, about a year later, she thrust out a rigid right arm and kept me a good four feet away from her. She need not have worried. I had learned my lesson. But I still wonder how world leaders figure out how many kisses to give when they meet their counterparts. It seems as if caution and a conservative approach are called for when greeting acquaintances!

Travel never ceases to reward, whether it is in a far-flung exotic enclave or down the road with our country cousins. When it comes to coping with stress, we all need a change of scene as often as we can manage it. Even a bargain weekend break in a midlands hotel can do a lot to refresh our minds and bodies, away from the humdrum of the daily routine. My list of benefits accrued from travel could be endless. Here are some of my favourites:

◊ Travel clears your head of so much unnecessary baggage.

◊ It gives you a fresh start in taking on the inevitable challenges around you.

◊ It enhances relationships with friends or family who live away from home.

◊ It can provide a complete change of perspective.

◊ Travel lifts you out of whatever shell you may be residing under.

◊ It provides distance from any difficult circumstances you may be dealing with at the time.

◊ A change of scene inevitably has a calming effect on our whole system, both physically and mentally.

◊ It compels us to take a rest.

◊ You meet lots of new and very interesting people.

◊ You learn to appreciate all the wonderful aspects of home.

◊ Travel broadens the mind.

◊ You come back from your travel experience with a renewed sense of purpose.

◊ You learn to appreciate the many differences (and similarities) between your own culture and the one you have just visited.

◊ It provides you with dinner party stories for the next two years! (a benefit not to be underestimated).

◊ Travel is great fun.

◊ If travelling alone you will inevitably develop resourcefulness.

◊ You are likely to try things you have never done before and certainly would not attempt at home (such as the dreaded bungee jump!).

◊ You create memories that last for generations.

◊ Travel is probably the greatest learning experience of all.

◊ It enhances our capacity to appreciate the beauty that surrounds us everywhere.

Travel adds to our collective life experience in ways that do not lend themselves to the written word. Those of us fortunate to have been able to see other places understand this. To deal with the stresses of your daily routine, allow yourself the opportunity for a change of perspective. As the cost of travelling has significantly reduced in the past decade, it has made it that much more affordable. So, no excuses! I hope I have convinced you. Go travel!

18

Sparkle

*'From the gut comes the strut, and
where hunger reigns, strength abstains.'*
– François Rabelais

The saying 'Fake it till you make it' has been around for a while. But what does it actually mean? Scientists from the world of psychology reliably inform us that if we make the effort to look and feel at our best, our brains and bodies respond accordingly. That is, if we act as if we are the most important person in the world, the brain receives this message and produces the feel-good chemicals that reinforce this belief. One research project demonstrated that if subjects adopted a 'high-power pose (such as back straight and open posture)' for just two minutes, this produced chemicals such as testosterone which are associated with feeling positive. On the other hand, when the subject adopted 'low-power poses (such as arms folded)' for the same amount of time, they produced chemicals such as cortisol which is associated with stress. The diagram below expands on the various benefits of adopting a positive mindset.

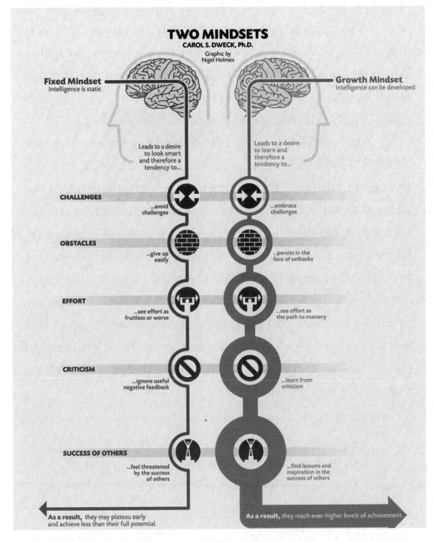

So there is clear evidence that if you make the effort to act in a positive way, you will actually feel better. And even if you are coming from a starting point of feeling stressed or depressed, there is further evidence that you can train your brain to be more positive. Even if you have had an unhappy childhood or have been bullied somewhere along your life's path, the evidence is there that says you can retrain your brain by acting in a positive way. The renowned researcher Martin Seligman outlines this process in his book *Learned Optimism: How to Change Your Mind and Your Life*. He argues that: 'A pessimistic attitude may seem so deeply rooted as to be permanent... [but] I have found that pessimism is escapable. Pessimists can in fact learn to be optimists, and not through mindless devices like whistling a happy tune or mouthing platitudes...but by learning a new set of cognitive skills.'

If you have developed a negative mindset over the years, which I would suggest is a particularly Irish trait, it is not too late to change. This is a decision we have to make. If we adopt a negative stance, our brains will produce the chemicals to match it. On the other hand, if you want to feel at your best, adopt an attitude that matches that. The brain is just waiting to receive that message and it can respond by producing happy chemicals. The message is to plan to sparkle every single day. From the moment you wake up, make the determination that you are going to look and feel great, even though this might not be the case as you fall out of bed. Follow these guidelines and you are well on your way:

◊ **Strut.** Strike that pose. Walk tall. Imagine you are a model on a catwalk. Straighten your back. Smile at people. Believe in yourself. You are unique. You are special. Step out as if you are a sought-after celebrity. Talk to others confidently. Be completely positive.

◊ **Wear** your good clothes. Aim to look your best every single day. You know the way we tend to keep that good pair of knickers in the drawer for special occasions. Get them out today. The same goes for the good top that has been gathering dust for the past year waiting for that elusive moment. Or treat yourself to a designer brand item exactly because you are worth it. The cut-price outlets make that affordable. Invest in good clothes that make you feel special. Wear make-up if you feel it improves your appearance. Change your hairstyle. Have your nails done. It has even been shown that if you wear formal clothes you perform better on intellectual tasks. So by looking your best you will feel your best and perform at your best. Do it now.

◊ **Dream**. Imagine what your ideal activity would be. Picture yourself in a situation where you would be at your best. Where is it? What are you doing? Who is there? And if that scenario is not immediately available to you, make plans for it to happen in the near future. Even if St. Tropez is beyond your budget, Bray is quite nice as well!

◊ **Imitate**. By copying how your role models behave, you will learn how to be like them. Who in your world do you look up to? How do you know that they are confident? What qualities do you admire in them? By trying to emulate them, you will start to be like them. Just don't choose Simon Cowell as the one you want to emulate! Pick someone you respect and who has values similar to your own. Copy them!

◊ **Create**. Aim to get the creative juices flowing in your brain. When we spend most of our time meeting our daily obligations there is less and less time to develop our artistic side. This is the much-neglected right side of our brain. Give your creative side an airing and pursue a creative activity such as painting or crafts. Not only will it be enjoyable but it will go a long way to keeping you feeling balanced and in control.

◊ **Oppose** your tendency to be negative. For some strange reason, many of us seem to enjoy wallowing in self-pity. When something goes wrong we see it as an affirmation of what bad people we are. The truth is that we have it in our gift to change that type of self-talk. Simply put, stop it! Do the opposite of what you are inclined to think and choose a totally positive interpretation instead. Remember, it is a choice.

◊ **Wash**. When we are feeling stressed or a bit low in ourselves, there can be a tendency to neglect some of our maintenance routines such as showering every day. Having a good shower or bath is a great way to feel better about ourselves. And buy that nice shampoo or shower gel. You will rarely come out of a shower feeling the same as when you went in to it. Wash away the stress and bring on the shine.

◊ **Nourish**. In order to feel our best we have to nourish both body and soul. Make the time to plan your look. Ask someone to help you. Take part in some type of meditative practice. Consume the foods and drinks which make you feel better. Listen to beautiful music. Feed both body and soul to be at your best.

◊ **Loosen up**. Life's challenges can cause us to become stressed without even realising it. Make a conscious effort to take a more relaxed approach. Imagine you live in California! Step back and look for the humour in what is in front of you and practise some kind of meditative/relaxation activity.

Any effort you put into making yourself look and feel better will be rewarded tenfold. Even if you do not feel like it, take that step!

19

Meditate

*'Meditation, because some questions cannot be
answered by Google'*

Meditation has been practised since antiquity as a component of numerous religious traditions and beliefs,
although it is not exclusively a religious practice. Meditation
involves an internal effort to regulate the mind in some way. It
is often used to clear the mind and ease many health concerns,
such as high blood pressure, depression and anxiety.

Meditation is beneficial for all of us. In discussing all matters relating to stress with Professor Ian Robertson, Head of Psychology at Trinity College, one of his strongest points was that every child should learn some type of meditative practice. It should be incorporated into the daily routine just as we brush our teeth or sit down for a meal.

It is difficult to find an exact definition of meditation but the following is one that comes close to describing it: The term *meditation* refers to a broad variety of practices that includes techniques designed to promote relaxation, build internal energy or life force (*qi*, *ki*, *prana*, etc.) and develop compassion, love, patience, generosity, and forgiveness. There are many ways to engage in meditation and some of the main ones practiced in the West include:

Yoga

There was a time when yoga was considered just another fad for alternative types who were rejecting Western religious traditions in favour of more esoteric practices. Thankfully, yoga has become very much mainstream and is practised just about everywhere. I urge anyone who is encountering stress in their lives to consider going to a yoga class. There are classes for all levels of ability from beginner to very experienced, and yoga is suitable for any age or body type. People may have an impression that only the very supple and lithe practise yoga. This is not the case. Yoga is for everyone. But it would be important to receive proper instruction before practicing it regularly.

Yoga came from India where it has been practised for centuries. It really took off in the West in the 1980s. There are various schools of yoga but by far the most popular form in the Western world is Hatha yoga. Essentially, yoga is a physical, mental and spiritual discipline. It consists of breathing exercises, stretching exercises which stimulate the glands to work in unison, meditation and dietary advice. Yoga takes a holistic approach, addressing all aspects of our general well-being. If you were to adopt the routines suggested at a yoga class, I am convinced you would see an improvement in the quality of your life and feel a greater sense of balance in most of your encounters with the world.

If it does nothing else, yoga makes you slow down. The breathing techniques it teaches are excellent for opening up the lungs and getting them working more effectively. The simple stretching exercises will get you striding out on your walks. The meditation aspect will bring you into the present, which is so essential when stress starts to get in on us. The dietary advice is generally very sound. This is not a fad diet regime but consists of suggestions for developing good eating habits. And the general sense of well-being is hard to put a price on. Try it!

Remember:

✪ Yoga is for everyone.

✪ There is a class starting near you. Seek it out!

✪ You don't need expensive equipment to practise yoga – just comfortable clothing and a mat.

✪ You do not have to have the body of a supermodel to practise yoga.

✪ Yoga can be practised for as little as 10 minutes a day.

✪ Yoga can lift you out of a negative cycle.

✪ Yoga has evolved over centuries of practice.

✪ Yoga includes very sound dietary advice.

✪ Yoga is not a cult as some people may mistakenly believe.

Progressive Muscle Relaxation

Progressive Muscle Relaxation (PMR) is a very simple but effective means of breaking the debilitating cycle of stress, through the use of a recorded 'exercise', which talks you through the process. It teaches the body to distinguish between a tense and an relaxed state. By training the muscles to relax, we can gain mastery over the messages the body is sending to the brain. So if our muscles are relaxed, the brain cannot be on high alert all the time. PMR can be practised daily for as few as seven minutes. It is possible to listen to recordings of any duration. Essentially, if you are going to practise it, the first step is to ensure you are in a relaxed position. You can sit or lie down as long as you are comfortable. The narrator then guides you through a series of tensing and relaxing of muscles, focusing on the main muscle groups. This is done slowly and gently. By the time you have completed the sequence, you will be in a much more relaxed frame of mind than before you started listening. As with anything, PMR requires practise. The more you practise, the more readily you will be able to call on this state of relaxation when you find yourself becoming tense. I firmly believe we should all practise PMR on a daily basis. It is very easy to do and is highly effective. Beaumont Hospital's Mindfulness and Relaxation Centre (www.beaumont.ie/marc) has an excellent website where you can access numerous narratives to match the type of meditation you would like to do.

Remember:

✪ There is a direct link between the mind and body.

✪ If we relax the body we can slow down the mind.

✪ Progressive Muscle Relaxation is a very effective method of relaxing the body.

✪ PMR is a simple method and be practised sitting down or standing up.

✪ There are plenty of PMR recordings available, of varying duration.

✪ With practice we can call on our ability to relax when we notice ourselves becoming stressed.

✪ PMR could and should be practised on a daily basis, particularly if you are going through a stressful time.

Mindfulness

This is a very simple form of meditation which has become very popular in the West over the past decade. It aims to get us to focus attention on both internal and external experiences in the present moment. We do this by focusing on our breathing and being aware of our senses. If your mind wanders during mindfulness meditation you are encouraged to accept this as part of the exercise and gently come back into the present. Mindfulness is about creating an awareness of the present. It has been found to be notably effective in reducing stress. Participants report that they feel much more in control of their thoughts when they engage in mindful meditation. You can read more about the benefits of mindfulness in the chapter titled 'Be'.

20

Stop

*'Life is a beautiful thing. Sometimes we need
to stop and smell the roses.'*

There are times in our lives when it is best to stop and do nothing. This applies to a range of situations. It is a strategy that should be considered as part of your armoury to cope with excessive stress. During the day take the time to stop everything and take in the moment. Resist the urge to keep going and instead observe what is happening right there and then.

The world famous American self-help guru, Anthony Robbins, was in Dublin not so long ago and gave a seminar to over 3,000 people. He started out with some very cogent observations about how we should live (he called it peak state) and how to get into the correct mindset. If we start criticising ourselves he advised us to say firmly to ourselves *'stop that shit'*. He got the full attention of the audience with that statement and it was one I will not forget. I agree with Mr. Robbins that we have to challenge negative thinking and we have to do so in a decisive manner.

I am sure that, with hindsight, many of us regret becoming involved in situations that turned out to be nasty, and wish that we had stopped before sticking in our two feet. Such situations are opportunities to use the *'Stop!'* strategy. Glasgow's Dr. Jim White emphasises this approach in his seminal 'Stress Control' programme. When confronted with a challenging situation, he advises thus:

◊   Stand back

◊   Pull back the blinkers

◊   Wait a minute.

By following this sequence we can make a far more rational response to whatever confronts us. Clearly, if we can develop the capacity to stop ourselves at any given moment, we will feel a lot more confident and in control. Here are some of the *Stop* strategies to consider:

◊   *Stop* 'catastrophising'. A common trait among many of us is to assume that the worst is going to happen. Challenge this standpoint and *get the facts!* Then deal with the reality rather than acting on your original flawed thinking.

◊ *Stop* self-criticism. We tend to be our own worst enemies and are often far more critical of ourselves than we would be of others. We have to learn to become our own best friend and be gentle with ourselves.

◊ *Stop* trying so hard. Are you a people pleaser? Many of us are. We aim to give far more than we receive. We have to balance this tendency to be the fixer every time. Are you the one who is always ferrying other people's kids to activities? Do you always take the minutes at meetings? How many committees are you on? It is actually more important to take care of yourself before looking after others.

◊ *Stop* reacting. The author Tony Swartz reminds us that the golden rule of triggers is: 'Whatever you feel compelled to do, don't'. In other words, we should resist the urge to come up with a response immediately. Dr. Steve Peters calls this our Inner Chimp (further details are in the chapter called 'Understand'). Reacting impulsively often produces the wrong result. It is triggered by an emotional reaction rather than a reasoned one.

◊ *Stop* for a few seconds. Consciously aim to slow down conversations, presentations, actions. For example, take a few breaths before starting to speak to an audience. They won't notice the difference and it will heighten attention. I recall a famous actor who, when asked for his greatest piece of advice to aspiring members of his profession, said it was 'the five seconds' – having the ability to wait, rather than diving in immediately, before delivering his lines gave him ownership of the stage.

◊ *Stop* doing the same thing. Remember Einstein's famous quote: 'Insanity is doing the same thing over and over again and expecting a different result.' While I don't think we are all going insane, I do believe many of us have this trait when attempting to find solutions to our problems. There is a certain comfort in familiarity but it can lead to inertia. We have to aim to try something different. While this can be daunting (doing something unfamiliar always is), it makes us feel alive. And it may provide the happy outcome to the challenge in front of us.

◊ *Stop* multi-tasking. We are only able to deal with one thing at a time. Despite this, multi-tasking is often the order of the day. Research has proven that multi-tasking is an inefficient use of time. By stopping and taking time to focus on one task at a time you will be using your time efficiently and will be less stressed as a result.

◊ *Stop*. Just stop. Take a moment to absorb all that is going on around you. What do you see? What do you hear? What is your body telling you? Make the time to do nothing for a few minutes each day. Notice every aspect of your surroundings. Be conscious that there are precious moments happening all the time. We just have to notice them.

◊ *Stop* to take stock. Pause every so often during your day to evaluate what you have achieved. We can sometimes feel that we are running at a standstill. We have to stop and review what we have done. By doing so we can see that there are lots of things, big and small, we have achieved throughout the day.

◊ *Stop* and do nothing. There are times when this is the best approach – don't rise to the bait! For example, I often advise parents that there are occasions when, rather than correct their children, the best strategy is to ignore. Doing this sends a very strong message to the child that you are not interested in them if they are misbehaving. This is a universal principle of behaviour – by not getting involved in undesirable exchanges with others; we are demonstrating good control and reducing our stress as a result. You will be amazed what a little silence now and then achieves.

◊ *Stop* procrastinating. We have a tendency to put off actions that are necessary. It can be fear of failure, fear of success or just being lazy that prevents us from completing tasks. Whatever the reason, we have to avoid putting things off because lingering responsibilities are stressful. It is far better to get the job done. Schedule the time, be specific and do it!

21

Listen

'The earth has music for those who listen'
– Shakespeare

We miss so much by forgetting to listen properly. Even in business, listening is widely acknowledged as the single most important skill to possess. And yet very few businessmen receive training in this necessary skill. We all need it. So much stress can be caused by misinterpreting information that comes our way or simply by failing to notice something which could alleviate much of our angst. We need to be aware that listening is a vital skill to have in our repertoire, both to feel in touch with our world and to generate solutions to our problems.

There are different situations in which we should remember to listen. Here are just a few:

Listen to Nature

Nature has so much to give – the sound of birdsong at sunrise, waves lapping on a shore, wind whistling through trees, or the silence of a glass lake in early morning. How often do we notice them? The next time you go for your walk, make a point of listening for the sounds of nature. It will bring you into the moment and enhance your walking experience. Don't miss it.

Listen to Your Body

Taking the time to listen to your body could well prevent problems. For example, a headache may well be your body telling you that you are dehydrated. A regular stomach ache may tell you that you are eating something that doesn't agree with you and that attention is required. Very often we ignore these warning signs. It is imperative that, if your body is telling you that something is not right, you get it checked out. A visit to the GP can eliminate a whole lot of unnecessary worry. Don't wait to allow the worry to take over. When in doubt, see your GP. We have to get better at listening and responding to bodily messages.

Listen to Your 'Gut' – Use Your Intuition

I believe our gut is a very reliable tool for evaluating situations. It is a means of communicating information which goes far beyond what we observe with our conscious mind. When our gut is talking, it is delving into the realm of the subconscious and the advice is usually very sound. So we should develop the capacity to listen to our gut.

Listen to Others

Various research studies indicate that only 7 per cent of communication is through words, 38 per cent is estimated to consist of voice tone, while 55 per cent is body language. The message here is that we listen with our eyes. How good a listener are you? Were you aware that the skill of listening requires so much observation? The renowned pianist Alfred Brendel is quoted as saying: 'The word "listen" contains the same letters as the word "silent".' That is the clue to good listening. It has been said that talking is repeating something that you already know. By listening, we can learn something new. By teaching ourselves how to listen, we are enriching our interpersonal skill set which will, in turn, boost our confidence. Listening is a subtle skill and involves more than being able to repeat to a person what they have just said (what used to be called 'active listening'). Here are some strategies to keep in mind:

◊ Establish eye contact. Make the person feel they are the only one in the room that matters. Looking around shows disrespect for the person. Good eye contact is a skill that has been attributed to some of the most charismatic people in the world. It requires practise and a relaxed approach but it is a very effective listening strategy.

◊ Adopt good body language. Establish the appropriate distance so the person does not feel you are invading their personal space, while still being close enough to make them feel they have your full attention. Orient your body towards them. Keep your arms open (folded arms can be interpreted as a lack of interest or being on the defensive), an upright posture and a positive demeanour.

◊ Observe the other person's body language. It will tell you a lot about how you are getting along with that person. If they are looking over your shoulder, the message is that they are more interested in someone or something else. Move on.

◊ Use gestures of approval such as nodding your head, changing your facial expression or giving a thumbs-up.

◊ Smile. The capacity to deliver a genuine smile is one of the most important personal attributes of all. (The chapter entitled 'Smile' goes into more detail on this pivotal skill.) A pleasant smile sends all the right messages to the person you are talking to. It relaxes them and also relaxes you, providing the basis for a very productive engagement.

◊ Listen for a person's name when you are introduced and use it frequently throughout the conversation. It is the ultimate affirmation to hear our name being mentioned by the person talking to us. We are instantly drawn towards them. Always try to remember the name of the person to whom you have been introduced.

◊ Interpret what they say. In doing so, you are showing that you have been listening and understanding what has been said. By getting this right you could be making a friend for life. If you do it in the context of a business meeting, it could be a deal clincher!

◊ Seek clarification. When you request that the person to whom you are talking explains their point further, it demonstrates interest on your part, and encourages them to keep talking (assuming that is what you want them to do!).

◊ Ask open-ended questions. They usually start with the letter 'w'. Who, what, why, where or when will invariably reassure the person talking to you that you are interested in them and what they have to say.

◊ Validate what you hear. 'Congratulations on your job promotion, you deserved it' will make you an instant friend – we all love to be validated and we never tire of it.

◊ Vary your tone of voice. A monotone voice conveys a message of boredom or disinterest. Aim to speak in animated tones to the person and they will feel that you are interested in the topic of discussion.

Listen to Music

Music truly does stir the soul. I read the following quote from an unknown author: 'Music speaks what cannot be expressed, soothes the mind and gives it rest, heals the heart and makes it whole, flows from heaven to the soul.' We cannot underestimate the power of music. It can lift us up from a dark place or soothe a troubled heart. Its impact is far-reaching. We have to incorporate music into any initiative to control symptoms of stress.

One type of music that is proving to be particularly effective for controlling stress is Alpha music. Research has shown a connection between Alpha waves in the brain and a relaxed mental state. It is well worth a listen if you or someone you know suffers from troublesome stress symptoms. It can be sampled easily on YouTube, for example.

Musical tastes vary and it comes down to personal preference. There is a whole range of relaxing music from Classical to New Age to choose from. Play your favourite rock music to lift your mood. Indeed, music can stir many different emotions. Whatever music does for you, let it flow. Just make sure to include it as part of your daily routine. It can change a tense atmosphere to a relaxed one in an instant. Do not underestimate its potential.

22

Sleep

'People who say they sleep like a baby usually haven't had one!'

'Don't give up on your dreams. Keep sleeping!'

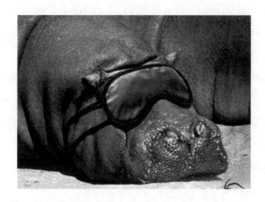

In the overall scheme of gaining control of our stress, sleep is the foundation for success. Without it, following through on many of the other recommendations for managing stress will be that much more challenging. With good sleep, we are well on our way to achieving the balance we all need in our lives. And yet we engage in many bad habits that make getting a good night's sleep more difficult. Do you drink tea or coffee before going to bed? Is there a TV in the bedroom? Do you enjoy a snack just before bedtime? It may become more obvious as you read this, but these are the very things which disrupt our sleep patterns. Another fundamental mistake many of us make is to sit up watching television when we would be far better off going to bed earlier and waking up earlier. It is said that the quality of sleep before midnight is superior to that after. An earlier bedtime would also enable you to wake earlier and enjoy the peace and serenity of early morning. This is when you could go for your walk or practise yoga in conditions conducive to relaxation. There is no more beautiful time of the day than early morning, yet many of us miss it.

The ideal is to get between 7 to 8 hours of sleep. (However, as we age, this requirement reduces because we are generally less active.) Many people have trouble getting a good night's sleep and there are different types of problems related to sleep. Some people find it difficult to get to sleep at the beginning of the night. Others find that they wake up in the middle of the night. Still others find that they wake up too early in the morning, particularly in the brightness of the summer months. Or perhaps you wake up feeling like you have hardly slept at all. If you have encountered any of these problematic sleep patterns, you are not alone, and you should act to change things.

When the quality of our sleep is poor it can become a self-perpetuating cycle of sleeping badly, telling ourselves we cannot sleep, becoming tense about it, and going to bed the next night feeling uptight and not being able to sleep. So fretting about poor sleep can make the problem worse, yet it is possible to break this cycle. With relatively minor adjustments to our routine, it is eminently possible to improve the quality of our sleep. But, as with any good advice, it is not enough to agree that it is a good idea. You must make a definite commitment and follow through on it.

Before looking at how to improve the quality of our sleep, we should be aware of what the sleep cycle looks like. We go through five stages of sleep in one cycle. Each cycle takes about ninety minutes so we complete this cycle four to five times in a night. Stage 1 sleep is very light; stages 2 and 3 are where our sleep becomes deeper. By Stage 4 we are in a deep sleep. The final stage, and the one where most dreams occur, is REM (Rapid Eye Movement) sleep. Our muscles become paralyzed and it is felt that the reason for this is to ensure we do not act out our dreams which could lead to all sorts of problems! It is important that we reach Stage 4 and REM sleep in order to benefit optimally from a good night's sleep.

Follow the pointers below for a better night's sleep:

◊ Make sure your bedroom is a relaxing area. It should be a haven of peace. Remember the senses when creating a relaxing ambience in the bedroom. Pictures of pleasant scenery or a happy family photo on the wall, lavender on the pillow, fresh sheets, low lighting. You get the idea.

◊ Remove any clutter from the bedroom. We have a tendency to store bags of 'stuff' around the bedroom floor. Try to keep the floor completely clear, including gym equipment!

◊ Do not have the room too hot or too cold. The ideal temperature is about 18 degrees (64 F).

◊ Have pastel colours on the walls. Do some research to find out which colours create a relaxing ambiance (see the chapter on 'Colourise').

◊ Use black-out blinds if there is too much light. It is easy to miss this important aspect of getting a good night's sleep. It is worth the investment to ensure that darkness is maintained at a consistent level throughout the night.

◊ No TV in the bedroom! Sorry, but it is too stimulating. Although some people feel that they could not go to sleep without the TV, I have to strongly disagree. TV is a stimulant and prevents us from having a good night's sleep.

◊ Avoid violent news or dramas on television before going up to bed.

◊ Buy an old-fashioned alarm clock and ban tablets and mobile phones from the bedroom – a midnight text or Facebook alert will ruin your night's sleep!

◊ Regular exercise promotes good sleep but try to take it at least two hours before bedtime. Your metabolism needs time to calm down after exercise.

◊ Avoid drinking too much liquid before bedtime to save too many trips to the toilet.

◊ Nicotine is a stimulant so avoid smoking before bedtime. If you have to smoke, try to have the last one at least three hours before bedtime.

◊ Alcohol disrupts sleep patterns. Avoid it if you want some quality sleep.

◊ Avoid all caffeine after 6.00 pm. Have a milky drink such as Ovaltine to relax before bed.

◊ Do not eat for two hours before bedtime.

◊ Listen to a relaxation CD before bed.

◊ Read only non-violent material. Some experts suggest not reading at all – you will have to decide what works best for you.

◊   Have a comfortable bed and change the sheets regularly.

◊   Go to bed between 10.00 pm and 11.00 pm.

◊   Have a nap during the day if needed. However, you may decide that you will only go to bed when you feel tired and, if so, avoid the daytime nap (see below).

◊   If your partner snores, ask her to sleep in a different room if that is possible! Okay him! On a more serious note, a partner who snores like the Concorde taking off will seriously impede the quality of your sleep. If there is a possible issue with sleep apnoea, it is well worth contacting your GP.

If none of the tips above works, try retraining your sleep as follows:

✪   Only go to bed when you feel tired.

✪   The bedroom can only be used for sleep. No TV, no mobile phone, no laptop, no computer games. (Sex with your partner promotes good sleep and is allowed!).

✪   If you are not asleep in 25 minutes, get up. Go to the living room until you feel tired again. Do not watch TV or consume anything.

✪   Keep repeating this cycle until you sleep through the night.

✪   Get up early in the morning. No later than 8.30 a.m.

✪   No naps during the day.

The importance of sleep in the context of maintaining an optimal level of stress cannot be overemphasised. But we have to work at it. You are probably aware of the different strategies mentioned. Your task is to now go and do them. It will make a huge difference to your general well-being.

23

Smile

'Making one person smile can change the world. Maybe not the whole world, but their world. Start small. Start now.'

'When I smile I feel good. When you smile, I feel much better.'

Before speaking at a seminar for graduating students, I listened to the talk given by the speaker before me. He was young man who has heading up the most successful Audi dealership in Europe. His business was based in Dublin and he had achieved this accolade in the teeth of our recession. He was relating his success story. I anticipated a presentation about his business model and marketing strategy. What he said left a lasting impression on me. There was one thing and one thing only to which he attributed his success. Every single one of his staff always greeted their customers with a smile. That was it. As a boss, he insisted on it. And his customers responded in kind by buying and driving away in their new luxury cars.

Closer to home, a friend of mine was diagnosed with breast cancer a few years ago. She described that awful first appointment to be assessed for her treatment. Anyone who has gone through the experience knows what it is like. You feel raw and completely vulnerable. My friend described how she went up to the reception desk at the hospital on that first day. The receptionist looked up, smiled, called her by her first name and assured her that the doctor would be with her shortly. That smile meant everything to her. It brought reassurance and coherence to a desolate and fearful experience. And it simply made her feel better. She knows this because there was a different receptionist at the desk for her second appointment. Without looking up the girl at the desk said 'What's your name? Take a seat' in one breath. The lady repeated the same grudging mantra to everyone who came to her. She made each one feel anonymous, small and afflicted. My friend had a totally different experience that day. It remains a low point on her cancer journey. And all for the lack of a smile. Thankfully, my friend had a very happy outcome to her treatment, but a difficult journey could have been made easier with nothing more than a friendly smile.

There is a considerable body of scientific evidence which emphasises the tremendous benefits of smiling. For example, if you meet a friend who smiles when they greet you, their brain produces happy chemicals (endorphins) as a result of messages sent to the brain by the muscles around the mouth responsible for creating a smile. You, in turn, will smile back activating further happy chemicals. So a very happy virtuous circle occurs, all as a result of smiling. The giving and receiving of a smile have benefits for both parties. Smiling has been shown to reduce anxiety, lower blood pressure and decrease the heart rate. It can lift us up out of a depressive fog. Smiling prompts us to recall happy memories and this inevitably prevents us from dwelling on less-happy times, which can happen when we are feeling stressed. On the contrary side, a frown causes the brain to produce cortisol, a chemical associated with stress.

Even when you don't feel like smiling but make yourself do it, there are benefits. The brain does not seem to differentiate between a natural smile and a forced smile. It still produces endorphins on the basis of the smiling muscles in our face sending a message to the brain. So even forcing a smile has been shown to reduce stress and boost morale. Smiling heals both mind and body. It has been shown that practising smiling will help us smile more effectively. Think of someone you love to put a genuine smile on your face. What does that feel like? Make opportunities to smile, even if it is at a tourist walking by or the cashier at the supermarket checkout.

One researcher has suggested that a smile creates happiness in the brain equivalent to 2,000 bars of chocolate. Now that is happy! And when we smile we lift the general mood of those around us. So smiling is contagious. It has been shown that people near us become more positive as a result of our smile.

Smiling can also trigger happy memories. For example, if you recognise a favourite tune coming through on the radio, your first reaction is to smile. The second reaction is to be transported immediately back to the time you first heard the music. All triggered by the smile.

Forensic psychologists have demonstrated that people who are lying tend to smile less. With hindsight, those who have been subsequently found guilty of committing a crime smile far less throughout the process than those who turn out to be innocent parties.

Anthropologists from Charles Darwin on have also noted the universality of a smile. While cultural nuances have been studied over the years, there is one gesture that is understood in even the remotest corners of the world. It is a symbol of welcome, of happiness and of friendship. When smiles are exchanged, even when there is no mutual language capacity, it breaks down barriers in an instant. Smiling seems to have been with us from the earliest stages of our evolution. It penetrates to our innermost instincts and creates universally positive outcomes. There are benefits for the giver and the receiver. So why don't we smile more?

Remember:

- ✪ A smile triggers happy chemicals in the brain.
- ✪ Smiling is contagious – if you smile, others will copy you.
- ✪ Smiling reduces the symptoms of stress.
- ✪ Even a forced smile sends the same message to the brain as a genuine one.
- ✪ People are drawn to those who smile.
- ✪ Smiling makes us feel good.
- ✪ Smiling makes others feel good.
- ✪ Smiling costs nothing!

24

Practise

'I found a book entitled How to be Successful at Everything. *It had only a single page and was just one word long – Practice.'*

'Practice does not make perfect. Perfect practice makes perfect.' – Vince Lombardi

My son was due to go into Temple Street Hospital for a minor operation when he was three years of age. About six weeks before he was due to go for surgery, we were called in for a run-through of what would happen from the time he arrived in the hospital to the time he left. He met the nurses, walked through the operating theatre, and saw the ward he would be staying in. He was also given a beautifully illustrated booklet which became obligatory night-time reading both before and after his surgery. Not only did my son tolerate every moment of his hospital stay, he thoroughly enjoyed it. All fear was removed through the innovative actions of the staff in getting him to practise the whole process, and the legacy of that hospital stay has endured to this day. My son has no fear of doctors, dentists or any professional, unlike my own generation who has never lost its fear of authority.

As adults, we are no different to children when it comes to being fearful of the unknown. And there is a solution. We have to train our brain as well as our body. This mental practice is a much underused strategy as we negotiate life's challenges. Many of us go through life dreading certain unavoidable obligations or activities. Public speaking, dealing with a bully at work, attending parent-teacher meetings or returning an item to a shop are just some examples of the type of encounters many of us dread. And, once again, how we speak to ourselves about this situation makes it far worse. 'I will make a show of myself' or 'I hate having to do this sort of thing' are just some of the negative things we say to ourselves. Conversely, if we learn to speak to ourselves positively about the situation, we can negotiate it in a much more satisfactory manner. 'I have something worthwhile to tell them', 'I have my rights' or 'I intend to sort this out properly' are the type of phrases to use. We can build our mental strength by making a positive statement of intent and getting rid of the self-criticism.

Let us take a look at one of the most commonly dreaded scenarios, a job interview. It can be daunting for even the most confident among us. You against up to five others, all firing questions at you. And it feels as if those who are not asking the questions are scrutinising you closely. So why on earth do we go into situations like this without practising? By sitting down with a friend and going through an interview rehearsal, you will take so much of the fear out of the actual interview. When the real interview comes around you will not be doing it for the first time. And you will have practised the various techniques outlined in this book to ensure that you give the best possible account of yourself. The same goes for any situation we find daunting – rather than dreading it, practise for it!

In contrast to the situations described above, imagine you were a tennis player or on a football team. Would you go out and play a championship match without any practice? How would you feel as you were about to start your match not having had any practice? Confident? Hardly. And yet we expect ourselves to perform these daily, awkward encounters without any rehearsal at all. Jim White, the eminent Glasgow psychologist, urges us to face our fears to manage our stress. One of the best ways of facing our fears is by practicing.

If you have to speak in public, practise it. If you have to face a bully or speak at a high-powered meeting, rehearse what you are going to say. If you are going to a parent-teacher meeting, write down your questions. And if you feel awkward about bringing an item back to a shop, role-play what you are going to say before going to the shop. The key is to take the unknown out of the situation. By being prepared we can reduce our dread significantly and lower our stress levels. Being prepared makes all the difference!

There is a whole body of science that shows how you can train your brain to deal with any situation you fear. It has been shown, for instance, that the neural pathways of the brain adapt and change when you undertake a new activity such as learning how to play a musical instrument or master a new language. With continued practice the brain develops new pathways to accommodate the new skill. So the more we practise for a difficult situation, the better we will perform. The brain makes sure we do.

Another important aspect to being prepared for challenging circumstances is physical fitness. Physical exercise benefits not just the body, but brain function also. People who exercise regularly (about 20 minutes a day most days) have been shown to create neural connections which result in them being able to learn faster and to be more alert. So we are going to be more able to face life's challenges if we train our bodies, in turn training our brains.

Food has an impact on our ability to cope with adversity. Interestingly, dark chocolate is thought to have a very positive influence on brain function. It is worth making the effort to include brain-boosting foods in your diet. Whole grains, oily fish, blueberries, pumpkin seeds, nuts and sage are all considered to be good for the brain. And they will help you face up to those feared scenarios with strength and confidence. So good nutrition is an integral part of practising properly.

Finally, it would be wise to take heed of Vince Lombardi's quote regarding practising perfectly. We can waste a lot of time pursuing the wrong objectives while practising. Practising does not need to take a long time. It should never be longer than 90 minutes. We have to be clear about what task it is we want to master and go about it in a measured and practical way. By doing so, we will be facing our challenges with confidence and just the right amount of stress to perform optimally.

Remember:

✪ We all have situations we do not look forward to.

✪ Our biggest fear is usually the unknown aspect of the situation.

✪ Good preparation takes the fear out of the situation - practise, role play, rehearse, prepare.

✪ We practise for sports so why not practise for life situations?

✪ Practise situations repeatedly until you feel confident about how you will tackle them.

✪ Teaching yourself to relax should be part of your practice.

✪ Face those fears! You will not regret it.

25

Exercise

'Warning: Exercise has been known to cause health and happiness.'

M ost people are aware of the physical benefits of exercise. But of even greater significance are the psychological benefits, particularly in the context of stress management. When we become stressed, and are perhaps heading in the direction of being depressed, the tendency is to move less. We might spend more time lounging in front of the TV or go to the pub to drown our sorrows. Comfort eating is not uncommon or taking to the bed can be the response of choice. Stress has a way of making us feel less inclined to move. But the one thing we have to do when we are feeling stressed is to get moving. The nasty thing about stress is that it causes various chemicals, particularly cortisol, to be released into our systems which slow the body down and make us feel worse. The good news is that when we take exercise we burn up these chemicals and produce happy ones such as endorphins, dopamine and serotonin. Endorphin means 'Endogenous Morphine'. It is a naturally-produced 'happy' chemical. It creates a natural high, which lifts mood and provides added energy. Perhaps this is why runners describe their chosen activity as being like a drug. Endorphins are feel-good drugs. They create a natural high in the body and a much more positive state of mind.

Endless research has been done on the psychological benefits of exercise. Most people recognise this. The challenge is getting to do it. In my own case, I can often come up with any number of reasons not to exercise. And sometimes I capitulate, don't go and feel worse as a result. But the one thing I do know is, no matter how bad I feel before taking exercise, I always feel better after it. There are many different sports and forms of exercise to choose from. Walking is probably the safest, cheapest and most effective exercise of all. (See the chapter called 'Walk'). Try something new if you have not yet found a form of exercise that you like. There is something to suit every level of fitness and ability:

Golf

'A good walk spoiled' is how Mark Twain described it. I have to disagree. I believe golf is a tremendous way to leave all your troubles behind and get lost in the fairways with nothing to worry about except your next shot. In order to play well you have to make yourself relax. The drawback is that golf is time-consuming and can be expensive. But it's well worth it, if you can afford both.

Running

The popularity of marathon running is testimony to the benefits of running. But there are options to run shorter distances for people of all levels of fitness. Most public parks have Saturday morning 5 km running/walking groups, which has led to a veritable boom in the numbers getting out exercising. Be part of it. It is not expensive to get started and you will meet people who are at the same level of fitness as you. It truly is a sport for everyone.

The Gym

Probably the only form of torture yet to be made illegal! Well not really. It can be hard to get motivated to go but it is always well worth the effort. It is advisable to get the advice of a qualified trainer about the best exercise regime for your needs. Those who embrace the gym are usually very contented and more productive in their everyday lives.

Team Games

It is said that rugby is a hooligan's game played by gentlemen and that soccer is a gentleman's game played by hooligans. And Gaelic games are hooligans' games played by hooligans! So maybe there is one to suit you among them! Sports clubs are the very fibre of our society and we should all embrace at least one of them. The camaraderie, the support, the discipline of being on a team, the fun to be had, interspersed with the rows, enrich the lives and communities of which they are a part. Don't miss it.

Cycling

This appears to be the current antidote to the male menopause. The number of lycra-clad men out on the road at the weekend is staggering. I'm not sure why it is virtually all middle aged men but it is clearly working for an awful lot of them. Give it a go if you feel like being part of an ever-growing sport.

Tennis

Once the preserve of the elite, tennis is now available to everyone. It is a great way to work all the muscles, expand the lungs and increase coordination. Tennis clubs are generally very sociable establishments, which certainly adds to this sport's attraction.

Dancing

There can be few more enjoyable forms of exercise than dancing. And it is a wonderful way of keeping fit. From ballroom to salsa, from zumba to pole dancing, the range of different dancing groups and classes is endless. You can easily join up no matter what level you are. Keeping a rhythm going over a period of time is a great way to expand the lungs and get the blood flowing. And there is great fun and camaraderie to be had while doing so.

There are many more sporting pursuits to choose from but you have the idea by now. Probably the best therapeutic strategy to cope with stress is to get some regular exercise. The recommended amount of exercise starting off is about half an hour most days. Joining a group will increase the likelihood of sticking at it, particularly in the early stages. There will always be a welcome for those starting up. If we are taking care of our physical health, our mental health will follow suit. Go to it!

Remember:

✪ Exercise improves our mental health as much as our physical health.

✪ Half an hour a day is what you should aim for, starting out.

- ✪ Try to get up early and gradually work up to an hour's worth of exercise.

- ✪ Exercise creates a natural and enduring 'high'.

- ✪ Exercise reduces the risk of heart disease, cancer, diabetes and many other chronic and life-threatening diseases.

- ✪ Join a club and expand your social circle.

- ✪ Walking is the most accessible and best exercise of all.

- ✪ Exercise makes you flexible and enhances your mobility.

- ✪ Arrange to exercise with a friend to keep you exercising regularly.

- ✪ Exercise oxygenates the body making it more efficient in the process.

- ✪ Team games promote camaraderie and discipline.

- ✪ Exercise promotes better sleep.

- ✪ Exercise helps detox the body, particularly the chemicals which are produced by stress.

- ✪ Exercise boosts the immune system.

- ✪ Exercise improves memory.

- ✪ Exercise makes us happy.

By now you will probably have gathered that I am a big advocate of getting sporty and active. There is an activity to suit every age and interest from rock climbing to lawn bowls. There are team games and individual games. There are games which take a short amount of time or which can go for days. Wherever you are in your personal life, however stressed you may be at this time, do something. You will not regret it. Getting active is the best stress manager of all.

26

Pray

'Lord, grant me the serenity to accept stupid people the way they are, the courage to maintain my self-control, and the wisdom to know if I act I will go to jail!'

"I told God to protect me from my enemies and I started losing friends!"

It was three hours before I was due to meet my friend for a game of tennis when the telephone rang. He regrettably informed me that he had to cancel the game because he had lost his wedding ring. He had searched all day and still had not found it. He was resigned to spending the rest of the evening scouring his home. I told him to pray to St. Anthony, patron saint of lost things, and he would find it. He rang me up an hour later and told me his wife had come home and found the ring in the washing machine. I assured him it was not his wife but St. Anthony. Our tennis game was on again, only to be cancelled due to a thunderstorm. Clearly, we had forgotten to pray to the saint responsible for good weather!

Prayer has been with us for over 5,000 years. It plays a significant role in every major religious movement and beyond. Meditative practices from various traditions incorporate prayer in their rituals. There seems to be an intrinsic need in most of us to speak to a higher power. Praying is expressed in a whole variety of ways. It can be done alone or in a group. It can be done in a whole range of body postures. In Native American culture dance is used as a means of prayer. Prayer can take place in one session or be practised across the day. People go to elaborate shrines to pray or they can pray at their work desk. There are any number of implements used to assist with praying, which seem to aid focus and concentration.

Clearly, there is a need for some order in the chaos of our lives. And it has been observed by many academics that even with the advance of science and increasing secularism, the human need to speak to a higher power has not diminished. In reality, it appears to have increased. And while views may differ on whether prayer has the power to heal, neurologists have demonstrated that people who pray for significant periods of time develop altered brain patterns, particularly in the frontal lobe region, which has responsibility for attention and compassion. From a practical point of view, prayer has a role in helping us cope with stress.

Some years ago I had the privilege to travel around Southern Mexico and I encountered a fascinating version of Catholicism. Different towns had completely different versions of how they practised their religion. In one town they combined worship of their favourite saint with praying to the sun. John the Baptist was the principal saint as he had baptised Jesus. Interestingly, baptism was the only sacrament they allowed in the church, which was run by the town council. So various saints had a shrine dedicated to them inside the church. If you had sins to confess, you did so via a mirror at your favourite saint's shrine, thus cutting out the middle man. When you had finished praying to your saint, you came outside to commune with the sun. This novel way of worship came about following the Spanish Inquisition when Catholicism was forced upon the population. The indigenous population found a novel way to maintain their traditions without being murdered for their be-liefs. So there are many different ways to reach out to a higher being, and this fundamental need has served humankind for a very long time.

Here are some of the benefits of prayer:

◊   It has a calming effect on a troubled mind.

◊   Prayer is a very simple and effective form of meditation.

◊   Prayer produces relaxing chemicals in the brain.

◊   Many claim that prayer heals them at a physical and meta-physical level.

◊   Even the knowledge that someone is praying for a person has benefits for the subject of the prayer.

◊   Prayer offers us the opportunity to take time out from our daily responsibilities.

◊   Appealing to a higher power helps us leave aside our wor-ries, even if it is only a temporary reprieve.

◊ Group prayer gives us a sense of community and solidarity.

◊ Prayer compels us to stop, reflect and slow down.

◊ Prayer reduces stress and anxiety.

◊ Prayer promotes a positive approach to life.

◊ Prayer helps us through traumatic times such as the loss of a loved one.

The famous atheist, Christopher Hitchins, has made a career out of criticising religious beliefs and even the folly of praying to a higher power. But he is missing the point. Prayer is a very personal concept. Every single person has a different interpretation of its meaning. If it is not your cup of tea, don't do it. If it is, go for it. And for the record, here are some patron saints that might come in handy one of these days:

Cause	Saint
Bodily ills	Our Lady of Lourdes
Assistance when all else fails	Jude
Stress relief	Padre Pio
Protection against bad weather	Eurosia
Heart patients	John of God
Women giving birth	Margaret of Antioch
Workers	Joseph
School teachers	St John Batist de la Salle
Mental illness	Dymphna
Innocent people	Raymond Nonnatus
Safe journey	Christopher

Dairy workers	Brigid of Ireland
Headaches	Teresa of Avila
Hairdressers	Martin de Porres
Hoarseness	Bernardine of Siena
Haemorrhoid sufferers	Fiachre
Senior citizens	Our Lady of Consolation
Bankers	Matthew

There is a saint for just about any cause.

Finally, prayer is a very personal thing. While it is a universal phenomenon, there are many different ways to practise. Find your God and have a chat with him or her. You will feel the better for it.

27

Help

'The best way to find yourself is to lose yourself in the service of others.' – Gandhi

'In helping others, we shall help ourselves, for whatever good we give out completes the circle and comes back to us.' – Flora Edwards

There was an unmarried man in his early forties who spent years campaigning to establish rights for disabled people, so that their families would not have to depend on charity. It was an uphill task as the plight of people with disabilities was a low priority for the politicians of the time. Eventually, a parents group from Limerick decided to stand a group of candidates in the General Election, and asked the man to put his name forward, and he agreed. It was a big commitment but one he felt was worthwhile. He ran a noble campaign but lost out to more established names. During the campaign he became friendly with a lady on his team. Their friendship blossomed and they married within nine months. They had two beautiful children and they are still together as I write this book. That middle-aged man was me! Some call this karma.

In life, if we remain exclusively self-interested, we will be much the worse off for it. When we help others we expand our own world, through new friendships, deeper relationships and the satisfaction of having made a difference. It is fascinating to see some of the wealthiest people in the world giving away most of their fortune and urging others to do the same. Warren Buffett and Bill Gates are among the most prominent billionaires who have made philanthropy their primary focus. Many wealthy people realise that their lives assume real meaning when they are helping those less fortunate. You don't have to be a billionaire to find meaning in giving. The evidence for the personal benefits of helping others is overwhelming. However, if self-promotion is the sole intention of volunteering in the first place, the effects will be limited. Getting involved in a cause is far more beneficial than simply throwing money at it. With that in mind it is worth reflecting on the positive impact we can have on our stress levels through helping others:

◊ **Distraction**. If you are fretting about different aspects of your own life, a good thing to do is to help someone else. By helping others you take your mind off your own issues.

◊ **Sense of purpose**. When we need a direction in life, volunteering to support those less fortunate can provide it.

◊ **Perspective**. It is all too easy to get caught up in the problems around you and forget that there is a wider world out there. By volunteering, you can very quickly see that there are people in circumstances much worse than your own.

◊ **Gratitude**. Volunteering provides a new perspective for when we are feeling sorry for ourselves. When we help people in need we often realise that we have a lot to be grateful for.

◊ **Social connection**. Volunteering provides an opportunity to meet new people. It has been shown that senior citizens can in particular benefit by giving their time and making these connections. Far too many people in their senior years seem to think that they have nothing to offer. In fact, they have a whole lifetime of experience to offer. This should not be underestimated.

◊ **Health**. Research has shown that helping others for between 100-200 hours per year lowers blood pressure and extends the lifespan. Helping others has also been shown to reduce stress and anxiety.

◊ **Brain power**. Other research has shown that volunteering activates the pleasure centres of the brain far more than when we are on the receiving end of kind deeds. So giving is better for us than receiving.

◊ **Career**. Volunteerism can help advance your career by teaching new skills and demonstrating your civic mindedness to potential employers.

◊ **Confidence**. By helping others we boost our self confidence.

◊ **Happiness**. It is an indisputable fact that when we help others we generate a significant amount of satisfaction from it. And, as we have learned elsewhere in the book, when we are happy, it triggers all sorts of physical and psychological benefits.

◊ **Fun**. Helping out is fun.

◊ **Relaxing**. The satisfaction we gain from making a difference in others' lives through volunteering can help us to attain a sense of relaxed calm within ourselves.

◊ **Motivation**. When we volunteer we can find new energy to achieve more in our own lives.

◊ **Optimism**. When we volunteer and join other people who give of themselves, we start to view the world as a better place.

I hope you are convinced by now. Giving is receiving. A few words of caution, however: First, make sure that you plan your voluntary effort well and that you get involved in something in which you have an interest. This will ensure that it is something you can sustain over time. Also, remember, in the words of a favourite phrase of mine, 'A good deed rarely goes unpunished'. A minority of people will always find fault with the efforts of others, no matter how well intended. Mother Teresa's poem below offers encouragement at times when the motive behind a good deed is questioned.

Mother Teresa's 'Anyway' Poem

People are often unreasonable, illogical and self centred;

Forgive them anyway.

If you are kind, people may accuse you of selfish, ulterior motives;

Be kind anyway.

Help

If you are successful, you will win some false friends and some true enemies;

Succeed anyway.

If you are honest and frank, people may cheat you;

Be honest and frank anyway.

What you spend years building, someone could destroy overnight;

Build anyway.

If you find serenity and happiness, they may be jealous;

Be happy anyway.

The good you do today, people will often forget tomorrow;

Do good anyway.

Give the world the best you have, and it may never be enough;

Give the world the best you've got anyway.

You see, in the final analysis, it is between you and your God;

It was never between you and them anyway.

28

De-Tech

'Life was much easier when Apple and Blackberry were just fruits.'

'Information is not knowledge'
– Albert Einstein

In a relatively short period of time technology has assumed such a place in our lives that it is becoming difficult to remember how things used to be before the so-called information age. When I was young (not all that long ago!) we had one phone in the house, and it was wired to the wall in the hall; in retrospect, a sign of its importance in daily life – you only braved the draughty hall when it was absolutely necessary to talk to someone distant. In contrast, homes these days often have no wired-in phone, but have enough mobiles to have one in each room. I was speaking to a friend in the UK the other day, on her landline, when her mobile rang – it was her son upstairs, asking her where his football shorts were! We probably all have similar anecdotes to laugh about, however, there is a serious side to the growth of technology in our daily lives. While it is now easy to be connected to even hundreds of people at any given time, it is debatable how much real communication is taking place. People can sometimes lose sight of the importance of talking face-to-face, because they are distracted by the various rings and pings of their mobile phone and are anxious to see who or what is looking for their attention. There's even a name for it – FOMO – fear of missing out!

So, for all our progress in connectivity, have our daily lives and relationships been improved by this progress? I would suggest not much. We seem to be more stressed today than ever before. Our lives are more complicated and our problems more rooted. People seem preoccupied with providing a running commentary on their lives, because they can. 'I'm sitting on the bus now'. 'I'm eating a chocolate bar'. Who cares? It is as if technology has tapped in to this fundamental need we all have for connectedness, but the volume of detail is as staggering as it is useless. Technology has also provided a means to witness first-hand just about every appalling atrocity in the trouble spots of the world. Do we really need all this detail? I believe we are being exposed to far too much information and it is not doing us any good. Apart from anything else, it distracts us from being present in our own lives.

Technology has made it possible to do several things at one time, yet researchers have debunked the myth of multi-tasking. It is not an efficient use of time since, when we multi-task, nothing gets done right. For example, it has been shown that the danger of talking on a mobile phone while driving is equivalent to driving drunk. Texting while driving increases the risk of having an accident by 23 times. So this constant connectedness has serious risks attached. And yet, we are linked in to numerous media at any given time. Texts, phone, e-mail, Facebook, Twitter, Instagram, gaming, music, and YouTube are just some of the possible contact points available around the clock. Connectivity never stops. There is more technology in today's mobile phones than in the computers used when they first landed men on the moon. .

While the technology has advanced, the etiquette around its use has not. Have you ever noticed someone checking their mobile as you are talking to them, or taking calls while you are eating together? The common courtesy that we traditionally expected seems to have become passé because of the anytime, anywhere access now afforded by technology. Another effect is that we seem to be in a permanent state of alert, anticipating a contact from another person, wondering why we've not been having contacts, or responding to one. And while the vast majority of e-mails we receive are of no consequence, there is always the anticipation that the next one might have some meaningful news. This constant state of alert is detrimental to our mental well-being and works against our ability to manage our stress levels. It is hard to see how anyone can be at their best when they are so frazzled with all this information floating around both inside and outside their heads.

Many academics are expressing concern about the shortened attention span among the technology generation. Attention Deficit Hyperactivity Disorder (ADHD) is becoming more commonplace as a result of constant connectivity. The

Diagnostic and Statistical Manual of Mental Disorders of the American Psychiatric Association (DSM-V), considered to be the Bible of diagnostic criteria, emphasises the link between the effects of technology and ADHD. Some of the characteristics of ADHD are outlined in DSM-V as follows:

◊   Often fails to give close attention to details or makes careless mistakes in schoolwork, work, or during other activities (e.g. overlooks or misses details, work is inaccurate).

◊   Often has difficulty sustaining attention in tasks or play activities (e.g., has difficulty remaining focused during lectures, conversations, or lengthy reading).

◊   Often does not seem to listen when spoken to directly (e.g., mind seems elsewhere, even in the absence of any obvious distraction).

◊   Often does not follow through on instructions and fails to finish school work, chores, or duties in the work place (e.g., starts tasks but quickly loses focus and is easily sidetracked).

◊   Often has difficulty organizing tasks and activities (e.g., difficulty managing sequential tasks; difficulty keeping materials and belongings in order; messy, disorganized work; has poor time management; fails to meet deadlines).

◊   Often avoids or is reluctant to engage in tasks that require sustained mental effort (e.g. schoolwork or homework; for older adolescents and adults, preparing reports, completing forms, reviewing lengthy papers).

◊   Often loses things necessary for tasks or activities (e.g., school materials, pencils, books, tools, wallets, keys, paperwork, eyeglasses, and mobile telephones).

◊ Is often easily distracted by extraneous stimuli (e.g., for older adolescents and adults may include unrelated thoughts).

◊ Is often forgetful in daily activities (e.g., doing chores, running errands; for older adolescents and adults, returning calls, paying bills, keeping appointments).

We have to be careful not to discard our values and our way of life in favour of the superficial connectedness of the information age. We nonetheless have to acknowledge that there are as many advantages as disadvantages to technology. As with so much about coping with stress, the aim is to get the balance right. With that in mind, here are some points to keep us from being overwhelmed by our new toys:

✪ Be aware that too much information is distracting.

✪ Disconnect from technology at every opportunity.

✪ Set aside specific periods of time for checking e-mail, and do not be tempted to check it at other times.

✪ Turn off your mobile phone at night. When was the last time you received a call in the middle of the night that was absolutely necessary?

✪ Make a point of having meals together at the kitchen table with all technology switched off.

✪ Limit TV time. Do you really need to see four episodes of *Say Yes to the Dress* or *Judge Judy*?

✪ Plan to complete one task at a time. Multi-tasking does not work.

✪ Never bring a mobile phone on your walk. That really is a good walk spoiled.

✪ Anyone who is studying must to do so without technological distractions.

✪ Make time for breathing exercises and meditation.

✪ Have a technology-free day every once in a while.

✪ Switch off the news.

> *'Small wonder our national spirit is husk empty.*
> *We have more information but less knowledge. More*
> *communication but less community. More goods but*
> *less goodwill. More of virtually everything save that*
> *which the human spirit requires. So distracted have we*
> *become sating this new need or that material appetite,*
> *we hardly noticed the departure of happiness.'*
> – Randall Robinson

29

Learn

'Live as if you were to die tomorrow. Learn as if you were to live forever.'– Gandhi

'Prioritise the fun and the learning will come'

In the previous chapter I outlined the negative aspects of the technological age and how these crowd our brains, impairing our focus, causing shorter attention span and diminishing our capacity for critical thinking. Well in this chapter, the focus is on the upside: the use of technology in the pursuit of learning. The Internet has opened up a whole world of possibilities to people of all ages and abilities. While books have been the main source of learning for centuries, and I hope we never dispense with them, technology has created new avenues to learning previously unavailable to large swathes of the population. Attending university is not now the only means by which to advance our knowledge. In the context of coping with stress, the pursuit of knowledge can be very helpful. Much of our stress stems from ignorance and we can address this through a commitment to learning. We should make learning a lifelong habit as there are numerous benefits to being informed, including:

◊ By being open to learning we are much more likely to find our innate abilities. Too many of us go through life with unfulfilled ambitions and potential. Never stop searching!

◊ By broadening our understanding of worldly issues, we become more adaptable to new situations.

◊ Widening our knowledge base enhances our wisdom. By understanding how others have negotiated life's challeng-es, we expand our wisdom to make choices in our own lives and to advise others.

◊ Learning teaches us the meaning and context of what is happening in our world. For example, by understanding cultural issues we can develop a more tolerant attitude to behaviours which may seem incompatible with our own social mores.

◊ Learning keeps us mentally sharp, fresh in our thinking and connected with the world. Numerous studies have endorsed the benefits of maintaining a lifelong learning approach.

◊ By becoming absorbed in a learning task we will reduce our stress. We cannot be fretting about mundane issues when our focus is on learning.

◊ Being informed means that we will have more confidence in social situations. Regardless of what topics you have studied, you can always incorporate what you have learned into a conversation.

◊ Learning offers perspective on the issues we must deal with in the course of our lives. It enhances creativity and the ability to tackle problems with greater authority.

There are many available sources of learning to set you on the path to expanding your knowledge base, including the following.

YouTube

If there is one new development that has opened a world of possibilities to all of us, it is YouTube. From the perspective of coping with stress, I strongly encourage people to avail of the huge range of relaxation videos it provides. From soft relaxing music to mindfulness meditation to yoga exercises for every level of ability, there is an endless array of useful resources. And if you don't like the instructor in your chosen video, you can simply go on to the next one. I particularly like the availability of Ted Talks on YouTube. These talks, which average about 15 minutes, are given by experts, and there are literally thousands of them on an endless range of topics. Keep your mind active and immerse yourself in a Ted Talk every now and then. (https://www.ted.com/)

Internet

It is now possible to complete a university degree on the Internet. Some may argue that distance learning is not the same as going to a university, but for people who cannot afford to go to a third-level institution or cannot access one for other reasons such as geographical or physical complications, the Internet fills a very important gap. As a resource for coping with stress, it is an invaluable tool. If nothing else, people learn that their symptoms are not unique to them. Even knowing that you are not alone in your stress can be a huge comfort.

Reading

There was a fear that, with the onset of the technological age, books would become obsolete. Thankfully, that has not proven to be the case. Apart from the information gained, whether fiction or nonfiction, reading is great for reducing stress. It is probably the number one activity people engage in when on holiday. Reading takes us away from our stressful issues and transports us into another world. Reading compels us to focus on one task which, in turn, enhances our ability to concentrate. And it is one of the most calming activities you could engage in. It is a fact that the more we read, the better we will be at writing (see the chapter on 'Writing'). And of course, reading books costs nothing – a trip to the local library will cater to just about any taste.

Classes

It is possible to attend classes on almost any topic. Every secondary school runs evening classes and should have something to stimulate your interest. If you are in doubt, just go! What have you got to lose? All of the great self-help gurus encourage us to take a chance. Try something different, they tell us. You may find a lost vocation by taking a course on a topic you have never studied before. You will meet new people and may even make new friends. And you will be able to ask questions directly to an expert, an asset which is unavailable on any other medium.

University

Previously the preserve of the elite, thankfully this is no longer the case. Universities have adapted so that people of all ages and with all kinds of disabilities can access their hallowed halls. They have become more complete seats of learning as a result. Universities also offer stimulating, informative evening classes (with no exams).

Clearly, the list above is not exhaustive. Regardless of what medium you choose, the first and most important asset is to be open to learning. Interestingly, the most successful people I know never went to university, but they never stopped learning.

30

Write

*'Either write something worth reading or do
something worth writing.'*
– Benjamin Franklin

'Sometimes only paper will listen to you.'

I once had a geography teacher whose lesson consisted of his reading aloud an entire chapter of the textbook verbatim. He then re-read most of the chapter aloud, this time having us underline the important points. Our homework was to write out everything we had underlined. If ever there was a misuse of the beautiful art of writing, this was it. At some level, that teacher must have recognised that writing helps to retain information, but he also turned 30 teenagers off geography!

While my story is probably not the best introduction to its merits, I believe that there are huge benefits to writing. An obvious one is that it aids retention of information, although probably not the way my teacher utilised it. Writing has significant therapeutic properties but to be of benefit, it has to be an enjoyable pursuit. It is a skill we need to nurture and practise often. This is particularly the case in the age of texting and computer spell checks. We are becoming lazy with the use of our language, and the gadgets are in danger of taking over. And if we allow that to happen we will be losing a very necessary skill, which has particular application to coping with stress. Here are just some of the very positive attributes of developing a writing habit:

◊   Writing clears the mind. When we are focused on writing we keep other stresses out of our consciousness.

◊   Writing helps us concentrate. When we write we are training our brain to stay on one task at a time.

◊   Writing helps to express complex ideas more clearly. What might sound good in thought can be exposed more fully in the written form. One writer put it thus: 'Brains forgive fuzzy abstractions, prose does not.'

◊   Writing helps us keep track of our ideas. According to one expert, 'Getting important ideas down alleviates the stress of losing your thoughts to time or an overcrowded mind.' In this age of frenetic time management, this is a particularly relevant skill.

◊   Writing makes us better listeners. A journalist friend of mine is the best listener I know. I love talking to him because he really seems to care about what I have to say. Did his listening ability come before the writing ability? Or was it the reverse? Regardless, his ability to listen is probably why he is so good at his job. If we write as a matter of habit, we invariably become better listeners.

◊ Writing expands our vocabulary, which is particularly important for people in their senior years.

◊ Writing, as a form of self expression, lifts our mood and reduces stress.

◊ Writing is a great way to clarify our thoughts. It slows us down and prevents us from jumping to conclusions. Writing creates a slower rhythm which means that our thinking becomes more measured.

◊ Writing stimulates memory. By shifting our focus to a specific topic, rather than juggling a dozen different issues at the same time (a common but not particularly helpful scenario), we free our mind to be able to recall past events with greater clarity.

◊ Writing is a workout for the mind! Just as we are encouraged to keep our bodies in shape, we also have to keep our mind exercised.

◊ Writing is relaxing. Even though many of us have gotten out of the habit, writing is a great way to take some time out for reflection.

◊ Writing makes us more ordered in our thinking. A certain amount of planning takes place when we write. As we develop this skill, it has the very useful knock-on effect of making us better at problem-solving and planning.

◊ Writing is, I believe, a great way of learning, regardless of the story I related from my school days! A student who develops the habit of summarising material in writing has a far greater chance of holding that information in their memory, whether it is for an exam or for a life skill to be used at a later date.

◊ Writing promotes creativity. It is a different discipline to talking. It is the expression of our creative thinking which will endure and can be built upon over time.

◊ With practice, writing can almost serve the same function as meditation. To create the best conditions for writing, it is necessary to clear away as many distractions as possible. The quieter the environment, the more conducive it will be for calm reflection and a more satisfying writing experience.

◊ Writing helps us retain ideas and information. A lot of brain power can be wasted by trying to remember information. I have discovered that I can only remember four items in my head when my wife sends me to the supermarket. Any more than that and I am on the phone from the shop to be reminded. Take the headache out of your daily routines and write the information down at every opportunity.

So how do we get started? Here are some ideas:

Keep a Journal

Some experts suggest that we should get into the habit of writing a journal every day. This does not suit everybody. Write in a journal when you feel like it. If there is something bothering you, get it down on paper. But don't forget to write down something for which you are grateful too. Keeping a journal is considered to be a very useful mindfulness exercise, and there is a direct connection between mindfulness and feeling happier. It is also considered to be a very healing activity, allowing us to purge bad memories and savour good ones. And keeping a journal boosts our self-confidence by compelling us to relive our successes during the day. Even Oprah Winfrey has touted the benefits of keeping a journal.

Set Goals

Various research studies have shown that if we get into the habit of writing out our goals we will be healthier and happier as a result. When we clarify our priorities we are less likely to feel overwhelmed and will thereby reduce our stress levels. See the chapter called 'Plan' for some worksheets to assist in writing out your goals.

Send Cards

How often do you get a handwritten card through the letter-box? Not very often, right? And yet we love to receive a nice card. It connects us to the sender and gives us a warm feeling to know we are being thought about. So write that Thank You card or the one that simply says you are thinking about the person. Avoid the e-card route as it just seems impersonal - make the effort and write.

Keep a Diary

I am surprised at the number of people who do not use a diary to plan and keep track of their time. Give your brain a rest and avoid the stress of trying to remember when and where you are meant to be at any given time. Take time to choose a diary format that will work for you. Make the diary your friend and you will find that it will help you to keep on track.

Write your Story

We all have a story to tell. And I have no doubt your story is more interesting than a celebrity writing about their drug hell or their five divorces. By writing your own story you get to know yourself and to appreciate what you have achieved in life – we all need to do that every once in a while. It is also a great legacy for your children, even before you have passed on.

Make Resolutions

They say that most of us break our New Year's resolutions by the end of January. I still think it is a good idea to make them. Having made our resolutions, we are more likely to stick to them if we review them at the end of each month. Check on progress and perhaps make a plan on how to advance one or two of them. If nothing else, yearly resolutions give us a sense of direction and keep us in touch with our long-term ambitions.

Blog

While I freely admit to being a bit of a Luddite, I concede that creating a blog is an ideal way for some people to satisfy their urge to write. It can also allow them to reach a wider group who share their interests, and perhaps to forge new friend-ships.

Write a Letter

Write to your public representative. Write to your friends (a hand-written letter will be particularly well received). Write to people you admire. Expressing your feelings about an issue or a person in written form can be liberating. If you are angry with someone but do not want to get into a row, or cannot ex-press it to them, write a letter to get it off your chest and then destroy it. The act of getting your feelings down on paper can lower blood pressure.

31

Simplify

'Everything should be made as simple as possible. But not simpler' – Albert Einstein

'If you can't explain it to a six year old, you don't understand it yourself' – Einstein again

'Simplicity is the ultimate sophistication' – Leonardo da Vinci

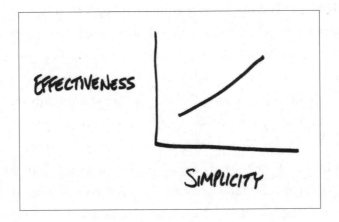

It had always been my wish that if I ever had children, I would take them to Disneyland. When the first part of my wish was joyfully realised, I enthusiastically planned the trip. When they were aged two and four we booked the trip to Paris

and on to meet Mickey. My dream was complete and here we were in 'the happiest place on earth'. However, I have to confess that the only ride my children wanted to go on for the whole trip was the three-horse carousel in the hotel lobby. My bubble was truly popped when I tried to convince them they would love the Peter Pan ride and they asked to go back to the hotel. It was then I discovered that children have so much to teach us. Glitzy theme parks and preconceived notions on my part did not make a good combination.

I should have learned that lesson from my own childhood. We never had a car when I was growing up. There was always great excitement when Oliver (a work colleague of my father) showed up with his estate car to our home just outside Dublin city near Cabra to take us to our holiday by the sea. Budgies in cages, dogs and even children were loaded up. We were the celebrities of the hour in the neighbourhood and waved to our friends as if we were Jules Verne and his entourage departing for a trip around the world. We were going all of nine miles to Malahide! Having been fortunate enough to travel to most corners of the world since then, I don't think the excitement of leaving for Malahide every summer has ever been matched.

There was so much richness in the simplicity of our lives then. I believe it is a simplicity all of us should aim for. The technological age has fried our brains and ramped up our stress levels. We never seem to be able to relax as we check e-mail, scan Facebook, respond to Twitter, text our friends and report on the latest rasher we have just consumed. It is high time that we claimed back the simple lifestyle enjoyed by previous generations. Our mental health will certainly be the better for it. There is endless research confirming the necessity of returning to a simpler way of life.

I find myself saying 'less is more' to my clients virtually every day, and in reference to a whole range of different situations. Simplicity makes everything manageable. And while the need to simplify matters is often very clear, it is not always so straightforward to accomplish it. We have to begin any task with the intention of keeping things simple and maintain that objective at all times. In a letter to a friend, Mark Twain apologised for writing such a long letter because he hadn't had time to write a shorter one. The late Steve Jobs, founder of Apple, was an advocate of simplicity when he said, 'You have to work hard to get your thinking clean to make it simple. But it's worth it in the end because once you get there, you can move mountains.' Simplicity clears our minds and makes us more creative.

It is often the simple things that create the most lasting memories. What are your favourite memories of Christmases past? Perhaps it is mixing the pudding with your mother, cheating at Monopoly or decorating the Christmas tree. It is unlikely to be how expensive your Christmas presents were. In more recent times, however, many parents have tended to engage in a frenzied pursuit of the current fad toy. The gardaí were called to one toy shop last year as two parents fought over the last 'must have' item on the shelf! There wasn't too much good will in evidence that day! Remember that happiness does not equate to the amount of money spent. Perhaps Christmas should be an opportunity to teach our children about what really is important in life, without being a killjoy, of course! While it is difficult to resist the marketing messages that seem to confront us at every turn, we have to fight the machine and get in touch with what really matters in our lives. We have to expose our children to the beauty of simplicity and start to notice what is around us. Indeed, we have to do that for ourselves. Make a start by doing the following:

◊ **Declutter**. While it might be too tall an order to create a minimalist environment in your home (even if you wanted to!), aim to get rid of unnecessary 'stuff' every week, and resist replacing it with more. If you feel bad throwing out perfectly good things, give them to your local charity shop or recycling centre instead. The effect of clearing clutter on our sense of well-being is remarkable and helps us to feel less cluttered in our brain. Enlist the help of friends or relatives if you feel you cannot do it alone.

◊ **Use simple language** in both the written and spoken word. This creates clarity and effective communication. Never embellish your words any more than is necessary.

◊ **Take small steps**. The longest journey starts with a single step. Take one at a time.

◊ **Operate the KISS principle** (Keep It Short and Simple).

◊ **Fight against consumerism**. Do not be a slave to cynical marketers. Teach your children to think for themselves and to avoid being slaves to slick advertising practices.

◊ **Simplify life by doing lots of free things**, instead of putting financial burdens on yourself to be entertained. Visiting the beach, the library or going to public parks are great ways to relax and don't carry a big price tag.

◊ **Walk, cycle or run** instead of driving or commuting by public transport.

◊ **Keep a work-life balance**. Make sure you do not miss a single family event by being overcommitted to your work.

◊ **Follow the rhythms of nature**, and enjoy the beauty around you.

◊ **Reclaim home-making**. Bake a cake from scratch, knit, sew, crochet, make jam or chutney, arrange flowers, or drink out of the good china. Re-engage with life's simple pleasures.

◊ **Make time for you**. Have a relaxing bath, go for a walk, read a book, meet your friends for a drink.

◊ **Actively pursue a simple lifestyle** and embrace the sense of freedom this brings you.

◊ **Try to be very concrete in your thinking** in order to cut to the essentials of whatever situation you are confronting.

◊ **Do the things you love**, drop the things you don't.

◊ **Live frugally** and avoid overstretching your budget. Do you really need a Mercedes when a Skoda will do? Keep your life simple and live within your means.

◊ **Avoid perfectionism**, it gets too complicated. Settle for doing your best every time.

◊ **Pack light**. When you pack for holidays, take out half of what you loaded in before shutting your case.

◊ **Unburden yourself of technology** as far as possible. Have TV-free days, limit computer time, shut off your mobile phone. There is far too much distraction causing us significant levels of unnecessary stress.

◊ **Prioritise what is important** in your life.

◊ **Appreciate the mundane**. Start to notice it.

◊ **Eat at the** table with your family without electronic gadgets.

◊ **Enjoy your garden**. It provides untold pleasures.

◊ **Avoid being a pleaser**. It ultimately creates resentment and stress for you.

◊ **Have a routine** and stick to it.

◊ **Create moments of silence**. Do nothing for a few minutes.

We could debate whether or not the quality of our lives has improved as science has moved on. And there is much to be gained by keeping up with the trends. But there is much to be lost if we curtail or eliminate the simple things in our lives. I attended the local horticultural show recently where my daughter got first prize for her fairy cakes, her painting and a decorated boiled egg. It was a marvellous occasion and the atmosphere transported me back forty-five years, when I got a first for my 'garden in a biscuit tin'. The waft of floral perfumes as I entered the hall and the animated debates about whose sweet pea should have won, or the moistness of the winning tea brack, were so reminiscent of those more 'innocent' times. There was something so reassuring about being in the hall that day. We should all try to take the time to simplify our lives, even for short periods of time, and enjoy such uncomplicated bliss.

32

Challenge

'It is the first responsibility of every citizen to question authority.' – Benjamin Franklin

'The greatest pleasure in life is doing what people say you cannot do.'

'Don't limit your challenges. Challenge your limits.'

About three months after the 9/11 disaster, I met a man at my cousin's wedding who was working on the 68th floor of the second tower to be hit when the first tower was struck. As news filtered through as to what had happened at the first

tower, instructions were issued on the intercom that everyone was to remain calm and to stay where they were. The man told me that he decided to ignore the advice and began to make his way out of the building immediately. If he had not done so, he would not have been standing in front of me at the wedding. Sadly, many of his work colleagues did not make it. They were the ones who followed the instructions from the intercom.

While we cannot ignore so-called authority at every turn, we must maintain a questioning mind at all times. If we go through life passively accepting what people tell us or what we hear through the media, the world will become a more frustrating place. We have to stand up for our rights and take an active role in how we want to run our lives. By choosing to be more proactive, we make our lives more satisfying and less stressful. With practice, our confidence levels will increase. Make the decision now that you will no longer be walked upon and that you are going to take the controls of your life.

Challenge Yourself

Are you realising your full potential? If not, what could you do to begin to utilise your talents to the full. It might be that you have always wanted to learn to drive. Perhaps you have always yearned to earn a third level degree. Maybe you have not gone travelling because you were afraid to fly on an airplane. Take a moment to think about the things you would truly like to do and then look into how you could begin the process of doing them. And, most important of all, challenge any negative thinking that comes into your head. You must be gentle and supportive of yourself and avoid the all-too-easy self-criticism.

Challenge Others

Just as we should challenge ourselves to pursue our goals, we should challenge others to do the same. Indeed, if you take on a joint challenge, there is a greater likelihood that you will be successful in your endeavours. For example, teaming up with a friend to get fit will increase the chances that you will stick to the exercise regime as you won't want to let your partner down by pulling out of a training session.

Challenge Authority

We have seen a number of cases through the media of tragic medical circumstances which might have been avoided had the staff at the hospital listened to the family members. If only the voices of reason had not been ridiculed as we were walked into recession! And the battle over water charges is the people finally saying 'S*top*, we have had enough'. This was a very necessary next step for our mental health, if nothing else. It is imperative that people in positions of power are not endowed with divine status. The testosterone-charged world of power is far from a rational entity. It needs to be challenged at every turn.

Challenge Negativity

Could it be a cultural thing? We Irish seem to find the negative in most aspects of life. Many of the iconic plays written by our foremost playwrights deal with tragic events, with the protagonists dying or going mad by the end of the play. Maybe it is the Catholic influence. We are all damned if we don't repent our sins. The premise seems to be that we are bad in the first place. Perhaps it is the weather. Whatever causes it, we should be aware of our predisposition to be negative and challenge it.

For many of us, our default position seems to be that we are in the wrong all the time. I was at the gym recently and had just wiped down the piece of equipment I had used. The next person to come along started cleaning the same equipment.

My first thought was that I must have forgotten to change my shirt or that my deodorant was not working! But why wasn't my first thought that this person must have an obsessive compulsive disorder or a problem with sensitive skin? No, I had to start with myself and assumed that the problem lay with me. This is the type of thinking we must all change. The most effective way of challenging negativity is to do just that. Challenge it. Step back and look at how you are interpreting each situation. Interpret the situation in a way that does not start with you knocking yourself. Do not assume you are always in the wrong. It is much more likely that you are in the right.

Challenge Beliefs

We have first to determine what our beliefs are. Many of them have been ingrained from an early age. We should develop the capacity to challenge traditionally held beliefs. For instance, does every doctor know how to treat your child? Does every salesperson have your best interests at heart? Can we expect justice in the courts? It is only when we have difficulties in our encounters that we realise our beliefs are vulnerable. It can be a notably stressful experience to discover that our beliefs, which have been developed in our formative years, are not matched by reality.

In her book *Shattered Assumptions*, Ronnie Janoff-Bulman says that from an early age we grow up with three core beliefs or fundamental assumptions. They are:

◊   The world is benevolent.

◊   The world is meaningful.

◊   The self is worthy.

When we encounter injustice, as we inevitably will, these fundamental assumptions are shattered. Loss of a child, financial implosion, marital breakdown, serious physical injury and rape are just some of the setbacks people encounter in the course of their lives. Janoff-Bulman concludes her book thus: 'Trauma survivors no longer move through life unmindful of existence; they can more readily relish the good, for they know the bad all too well. They have made their peace with the inevitable shortcomings of our existence and have a new appreciation of life and a realisation of what is really important. The wisdom of maturity, which acknowledges the possibility that catastrophe will disrupt ordinary routine, replaces the ignorance of naiveté. And the trauma survivor emerges somewhat sadder, but considerably wiser'.

So our beliefs will change with our experience. Make sure you have the flexibility in your thinking to allow that to happen.

Challenge Bullies

I do not know a single household that has not been affected by bullying. It is estimated that about one in thirty people are serial bullies, or socialised psychopaths as I prefer to call them. On average, there would have been at least one in every classroom. Those same ones seem to go on to infiltrate the workplace. They are toxic. They are pathological liars. They are dangerous. They are corrupt. And they are incompetent. And, regrettably, they are the ones most likely to be promoted. It is as if those who make appointments view incompetent people as less of a threat to their authority and promote them. Good people are often mystified as to why they get overlooked for promotion. It is most likely because they are competent, popular, intelligent and conscientious. Be warned! The rest of us need to understand that bullies are dangerous people who can seriously damage both physical and mental health. They are also cowards who surround themselves with lackeys.

Bullies will claim victimhood if caught in the act of corruption or destroying good people. It is important to be aware of how dangerous these people can be. Bullies often win and our authorities have failed miserably to protect people of conscience who have been their targets over the years. We have seen numerous examples of that played out over the airwaves. So proceed with stealth as you challenge wrong-doing. While it is necessary to challenge the bullies, do so with great caution and a well-considered strategy.

Challenge Criticism

Always look for the evidence when someone is criticising you. Often, there will be no basis for it, or the fault does not warrant the amount of criticism levelled. People criticise others for a range of reasons. They could be stressed, jealous, tired, angry over something else, in pain or feeling left out. Sometimes the reason may not be so obvious. Before responding to criticism, try to contextualise what is going on with the other person. Train yourself not to react with further vitriol. In doing so, you will take charge of the situation. Have a response along the lines of, 'Where is your evidence?' Or you could interrupt their attack with, 'You seem to be off form today, is there something wrong?' That will certainly change the direction of the conversation. Just remember. Get the facts!

If you find yourself slipping into a negative frame of mind and start to make statements such as, 'I am always messing up' or, 'I can't seem to get anything right', stop for a moment and think about all the things you have done right in the past week. Make a list of them if you can. By challenging the evidence we can teach ourselves to be more positive and realistic in our evaluations. We need to talk ourselves out of a negative frame of mind. Be gentle with yourself. Be your own best friend. Never automatically assume that you are in the wrong.

33

Gravitate

'If someone isn't making you stronger they are making you weaker' – Tim Ferris

'Instead of wishing you were someone else, be proud of who you are. You never know who has been looking at you wishing they were you' – Alberto Caring

What makes life so interesting is the variety of people we encounter in the course of our journey. Some enhance our lives, others drag us down. The latter grouping can

tip the balance of our stress in the wrong direction. We need to be aware of this possibility and avoid slipping into a negative spiral.

If you want to have success in any aspect of your life, a good first step is to identify a person who embodies what you are looking for. It could be a person you know or it could be a famous person. Identify the characteristics you admire in them. Is it their values? Could it be how they carry themselves or simply their fashion sense? By acting like a person we aspire to be like, we will actually begin to be like them. It is a proven fact!

The highly successful psychologist and self-improvement author Dr. Paul McKenna takes this a step further in his books by telling his readers to visualise themselves as the person they wish to emulate. By imagining they are walking in the other person's shoes, Dr. McKenna says that they will start to behave like them. By focusing on this image while in a mildly hypnotic state, he suggests that we will become like the person we are imagining. It is a process that must be practised but he assures us it works.

Unfortunately, we can, at times, also be drawn to negative individuals. We somehow convince ourselves that they will change. We look away when their negative traits bare their ugly teeth. Or we abandon all objectivity and allow these people to walk all over us and continue to come back for more. It is worth reminding ourselves that we cannot change the behaviour of others, we can only change our own. We can improve our own life circumstances by making the right choices regarding the people with whom we keep company.

A friend of mine described to me that there are two types of people in the world: Radiators and Drains. People who make us feel better about ourselves and leave us with a warm feeling are the Radiators. Then there are those who make us feel tired and inadequate, negative and washed out. They are the Drains. We all know both kinds of people. In order to maintain our morale and keep our stress levels in balance, we should make it a daily objective to gravitate to the Radiators and to avoid the Drains. Decide which people are the positive people in your life, and aim to be around them. Many business manuals advise readers to be around the kind of people they aspire to be. This applies to all aspects of living.

Sometimes, however, it is impossible to avoid the toxic individual. You may have a difficult family member – after all, you did not pick them! You may be married to one or have a relative in the extended family who causes strife. You could have a bullying boss or colleague. At a minimum, you should aim to engage with these types of people only when they are being courteous to you. Ignore and avoid them when they are undermining your confidence. The first step is to recognise the impact they are having on you. Then decide how you are going to deal with them in a constructive way. Being aware of the draining influence of negative individuals should assist in organising your daily routines away from the Drains, spending much more time around the Radiators.

The best antidote to dealing with toxic people is to gravitate towards positive people. Look at your own reality. Are you being dragged down by the wrong people? Instead, start asking the following questions:

◊ Who are the people you admire in your life? Aim to work with them or socialise with them.

◊ Who are your role models? Where can you find similar people?

Positive people generally have a tremendous energy about them. They radiate positivity. They do not get overly exercised by negative happenings and are enthused by good things. They draw other positive people towards them. They laugh heartily and enjoy the moment. Equally, they are serious about things that matter. They are genuine, sincere and honest. They are the people we need to be around. Go and find them!

Characteristics of a positive role model:

◊ **Self-reliant**. They rarely, if ever, depend on others for acclaim. This is a very worthwhile trait to develop, particularly for lowering stress levels.

◊ **Integrity**. A rare enough commodity, but one that we must ultimately aim to take on board.

◊ **Confident**. Even when they do not feel confident, you will never know. They know how to strut! We need to copy that.

◊ **Unflappable**. They won't make a drama out of a crisis. They get the facts, problem-solve and learn from mistakes.

◊ **Passionate**. Our role models should be motivated and enthusiastic. Hopefully, it will rub off on you.

◊ **Committed**. Once a decision is made, it is followed through to completion. This includes having the ability to identify when something is not working.

◊ **Learner**. 'Leaders are readers'. An openness to learning is a worthy trait of our role model; not just from books but from life.

◊ **Flexible**. Being able to take a practical approach to life makes a difference. Life rarely happens in a straight line. We have to develop a capacity to adapt.

◊ **Connected**. Our role model should be a good communicator. That means not just being a good talker, but a good listener as well.

◊ **Balanced**. Ideally, we need to keep our lives in balance at all times. We do this by being able to step back and ensure that balance is maintained.

◊ **Kind**. Good role models are givers. They treat others and themselves with respect. They are aware of those less fortunate. But, in keeping with the previous point, they do so in a measured way. They avoid becoming martyrs to any cause.

◊ **Humility**. None of us should ever lose sight of the fact that fate has generally been kind to us. We should look up to those who possess this trait.

Remember:

✪ Aim to be selective about the people with whom you surround yourself.

✪ Decide who your role models are.

✪ Avoid toxic people.

✪ When you can't avoid toxic people limit your contact with them.

✪ Only respond to toxic people when they are courteous.

✪ Make it your life's mission to find positive influences.

✪ Be where positive people are.

✪ Befriend people of good character.

Footnote:

As I was writing this chapter, my twelve-year-old son asked me what I was writing about. I explained that it was all about moving towards the kind of people who make us feel better; the ones we look up to. I went on to explain that we have to avoid those who drain us of energy. He then asked me, 'What about the ones who have no friends and are not popular? We should look out for them too.' I have learned more about life from my children than any other source. So, yes, reserve some compassion, patience and understanding for those who may be on the margins of acceptability.

34

Love

*'Men are from Earth. Women are from Earth.
Deal with it.'* – George Carlin

*'Love your laugh, love your style, love your
heart, love your smile. Love your voice, love
everything about yourself.'*

Apsychiatrist once told me that half of his patients come to him because they are not married. The other half comes to him because they are! The dictionary tells us that love is 'a feeling of deep regard, fondness and devotion'. But it does not specify towards what. Love is something that we all seem to know when we feel it but have a very difficult time defining it. So where do we start? The call to 'Love' someone or something comes as a recommendation for coping with stress in this book, but I am struggling to say what it is. So much has been written about it but there is no good way to describe it.

What is absolutely certain is that the most important love is the love of oneself. We have to respect ourselves, invest in ourselves and be comfortable with ourselves. This will enhance our capacity to reach out and find something similar outside of ourselves. It is said that if we learn to love ourselves it opens up all sorts of possibilities. 'Happiness is loving yourself first, so that you can share that love with someone else' is how one person described it. One myth I want to challenge is the notion that the only way to find true love is through a long-term heterosexual union. There are different ways to find love and it all starts with the self.

Love Yourself

Life becomes less complicated when we start to appreciate ourselves. Much of how we view ourselves can be based on past experiences, even from our childhood years. But we cannot change that. What we can change is the present and how we are treated in the future. That has to be our focus. Try some of these to get you going:

◊ Be positive. Bin that tendency to be cynical and bitter. It is as simple as making the decision to do so.

◊ Have fun. Have a laugh. Go to a comedy night. Try something new.

◊ Accept yourself for who you are and not who you are going to be when you lose three stone or change the colour of your hair. There is no one like you on earth. Fact!

◊ Talk kindly to yourself. Go gently with your evaluation of how you are doing.

◊ Be your own Number 1 fan. Interestingly, people are drawn to others who evaluate themselves in a positive way.

◊ Never compare yourself with others. Chances are, they are comparing themselves with you, which is not a good idea either.

◊ View adversity as a necessary life experience. It is the best way to learn.

◊ Be patient with yourself. Take your time and be slow to reach conclusions.

◊ Smile more. That's all. It works.

◊ Praise yourself often. Rather than seek the acknowledgement of others, rely on your own positive appraisal instead. You have more control over that so make sure it is a good one.

◊ Work on your deficits. Instead of dismissing something as beyond your control, make plans to work on it and improve.

◊ Invest in yourself. As the ad says, 'because you're worth it'. Join a gym. Have a beauty treatment. Invest in good exercise equipment. Go to the night class you have been thinking about but never went. Keep this on your agenda every day.

◊ Try new things. Broaden your horizons and find out more about yourself. You will enjoy the process. It is that first step which is the most difficult. Take it!

◊ Laugh at yourself. Don't take yourself too seriously.

◊ Socialise. Make the effort and meet people. Invite people to your home if going out is not your cup of tea.

◊ Look your best every day. You will feel more confident and have more energy.

◊ Draw a line through the past. It is gone. We cannot change it. Move on.

◊ Stay healthy. It truly is our wealth. Make it a priority.

Love Your Family

Even though you did not pick them, you will find that family tend to be your most loyal friends. Who is there at times of adversity? Who is there at times of loss? Who is there to celebrate our most significant milestones in life? As I have aged I have grown to realise that true friends are there for you when life gets tough. And I could count on one hand the ones who were there outside my family. I don't think I am unique in that. We should aim to nurture our family relationships. Where there have been rifts, if it is possible at all, try to heal them. The song about a son's relationship with his father by Mike and the Mechanics, 'The Living Years', captures this sentiment perfectly: 'It's too late when we die, To admit we don't see eye to eye......I just wish I could have told him in the living years'. If it's not too late for you, go and do something about it now.

Love Your Pet

The former U.S. President Harry Truman is quoted as saying, 'If you want a friend in Washington, get a dog.' I believe his view of friendships and dogs goes far beyond the confines of Washington. Pets, and particularly dogs, have a tremendous role to play in our lives. There are any number of reasons why a dog is good for you. Research confirms that dog owners are happier and healthier. Owning a dog means you are less likely to have heart problems and if you do, a relapse is less likely. Having a dog means you have to exercise more as they require a daily walk. And reaching down to clean up the poo adds to the workout! In general, dogs reduce the stress levels in any household. And having a dog is also a great way to meet people! The type of pet you decide on is a personal choice. What is clear is that pets provide that unconditional love we all need and enjoy.

Love Your Partner

Before outlining how to love your partner, it is important to point out that having a partner is not the only ideal state in life. There are far too many single people who seem to feel that, because they are not in a settled relationship, there is something wrong with them. People who are single often perceive themselves as being surrounded by happily settled couples. A reality check is required here. Not all people are in relationships, and those that are may not be that happy. It is only single people who develop this notion that 'I am the only one ...'. I feel for people in their twenties and thirties when the mating game is at its height. Those who are not in ideal relationships (I don't know anyone who is) too often lament the kind of relationships hyped up through media outlets. Unconditional love and endless passion are mostly figments of the imagination of idealistic, and usually single, journalists and film makers. The unfortunate outcome of this is to make the vast majority of the population feel inadequate when it comes to their relationship status. Whether single or in a partnership, enjoy it. For those who are in a relationship and want to make it last, here are some ground rules:

✪ Don't have ground rules. Let the relationship evolve.

✪ Maintain a level of autonomy and independence.

✪ Be honest from the start.

✪ Don't confuse sex with love. It very often isn't.

✪ Be spontaneous. Do something unexpected for your partner every now and then.

✪ Share responsibilities.

✪ Talk to each other. This art can be lost as relationships
establish themselves.

✪ Negotiate issues which lack clarity. It could prevent a major row further down the line.

✪ Grow together. The person you met for the first time is
never going to be the same a year on and beyond. Enjoy
the process of growing together.

✪ Accept that your partner is not perfect. Love them warts
and all!

Love life. It is all we have. Embrace it. Notice it. Query it.
Love it.

35

Colourise

'Colour is like food for the spirit – plus it's not addictive or fattening.' – Isaac Mizrahi

'Colours are the smiles of nature'
– James Henry Leigh Hunt

Afriend of mine who is a doctor told me a story about when he was a student. The annual Medical Ball was on and the dress code was black and white. He did not have enough money to bring somebody with him so he went on his own. Imagine his shock when he arrived late into a ballroom full of his tuxedo-clad tutors and peers while he was dressed as a naughty nun! He decided to just keep going and made the most of the night anyway. So the message here is that colours can mean different things to different people. For me, black and white reminds me of when I played rugby on the Belvedere College Senior Cup Rugby team in 1979. Vivid memories still linger of our defeat in the first round to the eventual winners, Terenure College. For zebras, black and white means survival!

During my travels around the world, I am often struck by the important role colour has in different countries. The influence of colour can be culture-specific, even within the same country. I was very struck by the distinctive clothing of the women around Lake Atitlan in Guatemala. Each village had its own specific costume which the women wore every day. The women in one village wore predominantly brown costumes while in the next village they wore blue. The nearby market at Chichicastenango was a riot of colour but each woman had a very definite identity, solely determined by the colour of her dress. Nearer to home it has been observed that men tend to wear cold colours whereas women are more inclined to wear warmer ones. And a general rule of thumb for interior designers is that cooler colours create a calmer, more relaxed ambience while warmer colours are more stimulating and arousing.

I had intended to write this chapter about the soothing nature of certain colours. But the literature contradicts that notion. Personal preference, past experiences, a person's upbringing, cultural nuances and the weather are just some of the factors at play in the influence of colour on our well-being. For instance, people in cold climates are more likely to have a preference for warm colours, while the opposite is the case for those in warm climates. What can be stated with confidence is that colour does influence our moods. From a local perspective, what is it about Irish men that the only colours they seem to wear are black, brown or grey? Perhaps it is the rainy weather, the Catholic upbringing or being on the edge of Europe where they feel they don't have to make an effort. No matter where we are in our lives, it is important that we introduce colour to lift our mood and make us feel good about ourselves. As a starting point, below are some of the generally-observed associations with different colours:

Red

Lust, Power, Action, Energy, Passion, Excitement, Love. It is no coincidence that red is associated with excitement. Think Ferrari, Virgin Atlantic or Red Bull. Marketers often match the 'personality' of the company to a particular colour. Research has also shown that athletes or sports teams who wear red have a higher rate of success than those wearing other colours. For example, in sports such as boxing, when a close decision is required and it is up to the judges, they are far more likely to pick the boxer wearing red. Of course, red is the colour of love and we can see nothing else on St. Valentine's Day (although I usually give my wife daffodils!). And did you know, if you drive a red car, you are more likely to get a speeding ticket!

Blue

Cool, Masculine, Corporate, High Quality, Trust, Honesty, Competent, Peace, Tranquillity. Blue is the most popular colour of all. This is the colour to address stress and anxiety. It is calming and soothing. It promotes both mental and physical relaxation. It is the colour of the sky and the paler blues are associated with a sense of freedom. Darker blue also represents authority as can be seen in the uniforms of most police forces. But the overarching feature of blue in most of its hues is the sense of calm and peace it brings to a situation. Keep this in mind as you choose clothes and when deciding on colours for the interior of your house.

Green

Healing, Health, Renewal, Prosperity, Good Taste, Balance, Harmony, Growth, Envy, Ireland. Green is generally regarded as the colour of renewal. Obviously, it is the colour most associated with nature which conjures up ideas of nurturing, rejuvenation and energy. Green is the colour of Spring renewal. It is considered a sanctuary from stress and a restorer of energy. This is precisely what you get when you holiday in Ireland! Green brings balance and is considered to be at the equilibrium between the head and the heart. Green is also the colour of money which can be a good or a bad thing. Perhaps this is also why it is associated with envy and greed.

Yellow

Uplifting, Happiness, Competence, Optimistic, Wisdom, Logical, Cheerful, Jealousy. Yellow is the colour of enthusiasm for life. It is also most connected to the mind and intellect. Yellow is associated with new ideas and clarity of thought. Given that, it is very much aligned to the head and much less so the heart. Yellow is noted for its high visibility and is most used in road markings and high visibility wear. Yellow is most likely to prompt new ideas and thoughts.

Purple

Wealth, Spiritual, Quality, Richness, Originality, Fantasy, Creativity, Imagination, Humanitarian. Purple is most often involved in the creative arts. It is no surprise that it features heavily in Disney productions. It is associated with deeper thinking and philosophers refer to the transformation of the soul. Purple represents the future. From a psychological perspective, it calms the mind, creates mental balance and harmony between the mind and emotions. It can enhance a meditative experience.

Pink

Compassion, Nurturing, Feminine, Sophistication, Sincerity, Love, Tenderness, Hope. Pink combines the passion of red with the purity of white. It is a calming colour which alleviates anger and resentment. Pink is associated with unconditional love and taps into the child within us all. It is also associated with good health as exemplified by the phrase 'in the pink'.

Black

Power, Authority, Grief, Secrecy, Sophistication, Intimidation, Seduction, Expensive, Fear, Submission. If ever there was a colour of contrasts, black is it. Perhaps that is why it absorbs all colours in the absence of light. It is mysterious and unknown. It provides a refuge for those who want to keep emotions out of view. As such it is the colour of choice for teenagers as they negotiate the bumpy and vulnerable journey to adulthood. However, if there is too much black around, it is associated with depression. In a general sense, black represents the darker side of life. It is the colour people wear at funerals. Power and control, authority and fear are among its other trademarks. Alternatively, black is also the colour worn by fashionistas to symbolise sophistication or to cover their bulges! On its own it is not so attractive but with other colours can form the basis of seduction. In contrast it is the colour of submission to God for religious people such as priests and nuns.

White

Simplicity, Fairness, Cleanliness, Efficiency, Order, Equality, Independence, Purity, Happiness, Perfection, Peace. White represents new beginnings ('wiping the slate clean') and starting with a blank canvas. It is the colour of innocence as worn by little girls at their First Holy Communion and the traditional colour worn by a Western bride on her wedding day. It is also the colour of surrender. It symbolises the cleanliness, reassurance and efficiency of a doctor who wears the white coat. In some cultures, white is associated with death and mourning but the association is related to the passing from one life to a new one. Too much white is considered cold and sterile. At an emotional level, it refreshes and renews our energy.

Gold

Luxury, Value, Prestige, Quality, Elegance, Wisdom, Abundance, Beauty, Triumph, Sincerity, Success, Masculine. Gold has a universal property which signifies wealth. It provides richness and warmth, not just materially, but at an emotional and psychological level as well. It is considered to be a giving and generous colour. Gold inspires a deeper understanding of the self. Along with the colour purple, it is the colour of royalty. And, of course, gold is the colour of winners as coming first usually means you win a gold medal.

Silver

Soothing, Calming, Purifying, Feminine, Sophisticated, Scientific, Glamorous, Prosperity, Modern. Associated with the power of the moon which controls the ebb and flow of tide, silver is considered to be the balance between black and white. As such, it is considered to have the capacity to cleanse and renew mental, physical and emotional issues and can light the way forward. It is considered to be patient, organised, self-controlled and determined which makes it a match in the corporate world. Silver goes with most other colours and is the colour of the 25th anniversary of a couple's marriage.

Grey

Neutral, Conservative, Detached, Subdued, Conservative, Boring, Formal, Drab, Reliable, Conformist, Unemotional. .

On a positive note, the solidity of grey provides relief from an otherwise chaotic world. Grey is generally considered to tone down brighter colours and to illuminate softer ones. It is associated with sadness and depression. In certain brighter versions of it, grey can be interesting but the overall message is that grey lacks both energy and style.

Brown

Strong, Wholesome, Rugged, Outdoor, Reassuring, Grounded, Practical, Loyal, Honest, Sincere, Quality, Organic, Friendly. Brown has a down-to-earth quality with a clear association with the need for security and protection of those for whom we are responsible. Brown is also associated with material possessions. It is generally a common-sense colour, a very useful asset in the context of coping with stress. Along with green, it is the colour of nature so has a clear association with the outdoors. They are the two most common colours on the planet. Brown is considered a reassuring colour.

So there we have it. Outlined above are possible influences of some of the most basic colours on the spectrum. There are thousands of variations and combinations which can create a mood or an atmosphere. Keep in mind that there is a rich landscape of colours between black and white. Too much of any one thing can become dull or problematic. Aim to introduce lots of colour into your world. Make them bright, rich and thoughtful. A friend of mine told me that she took her children to a 5K colour run recently. At the start of the run everyone was given bags of different coloured chalk dust to throw over one another creating a riot of colour. They had an absolute ball that day. We should all do the same. Let colour loose. Whether it is clothes or interior design, cooking or flowers in the garden, bring colour into your life. You will feel the better for it.

36

Habituate

'We are what we repeatedly do. Excellence, then, is not an art, but a habit.' – Aristotle

'Bad habits are like a comfortable bed. Easy to get into, but hard to get out of.'

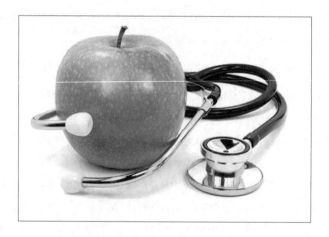

I was driving along with my daughter, who was five at the time, in the back seat. Our chats would normally be about whether Barney was a man or a women or why Dora the Explorer's parents never looked after her. But on this particular day she asked, 'Dad, is the brain a muscle?' I almost crashed the car. Where did that question come from? And the more I thought about it, the more brilliant a question I realised it was. And I didn't know the answer. I still need to get a proper explanation from one of my more learned colleagues. What I do know is that the brain certainly is an organ of the body. And it behaves like a muscle. The more we work it, the stronger it gets. When we work at it regularly, it forms neural pathways which facilitate the regular activity we undertake. An obvious example is when we learn to drive. At first, we have to think about every wheel turn and gear change. But after a while, the brain has had sufficient practice that we do it automatically.

Dr. Donal O'Shea, consultant in obesity, was talking on the radio about one of his patients who was overweight. To lose weight the man's only intervention was to determine that he would not buy a bar (or two) of chocolate when he stopped to fill up at a petrol station. He lost two stone in two months! The impact of developing good habits cannot be underestimated.

In his book *The Power of Habit*, Charles Duhigg describes how it is possible to change bad habits. We have to first identify what the triggers are for our bad habits (Cue) and then change our usual response to them (Routine). The objective is to replace the bad habit with one that proves equally appealing (Reward). He calls this the habit loop

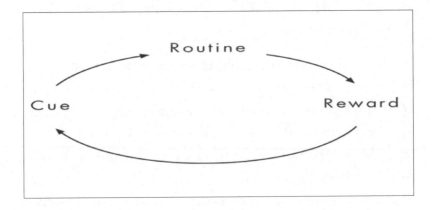

Duhigg outlines a four-stage process like this:

◊ Step 1: Our first task is to identify what habit loops we have in our lives. When do we go for coffee and a bun, for example? How do we react to stressful situations? Do we respond in a proactive way or do we capitulate to old or bad habits.

◊ Step 2: Change the usual reward to something more positive and healthy. Instead of reaching for coffee and cake, go for a walk. Instead of getting angry, breathe slowly and use frustrating circumstances as an opportunity to practise relaxation skills.

◊ Step 3: Identify the cues that lead you to bad habits. Is it the time of day, the company you are keeping or the absence of a proper routine? With some reflection, it is usually possible to identify what is leading you to self-destruct. Of course, we should not underestimate the power of marketing in influencing our decisions. Being aware of that fact may help with the next stage.

◊ Step 4: Have a plan to change bad habits into good ones. Eat an apple instead of a bar of chocolate. Go for a walk when you are tempted to drink more coffee. Plan for the times of day when you are most vulnerable to breaking your positive routines.

The brain is very adaptable. It can adjust to both good and bad habits. When we feel stressed it can be all too easy to lapse into bad habits. We may stop exercising, start to eat unhealthy comfort foods or engage in self-pity. These are choices we make and the message in this chapter is that it is possible to make alternative, positive choices. And these choices can establish themselves as habits in the same way as our previous bad choices. It is up to us to make the determination to develop these positive habits. Convention suggests that it takes 21 days to establish a habit. Decide what good habit you would like to develop and make your plan.

The brain and the body are similar when it comes to forming good habits. When we work out at a gym, the muscles are exercised and they develop. The brain is no different. So when we give the brain a workout, we have to make sure it is a positive one. The eminent psychologist William James, in his seminal tome *The Principles of Psychology*, used water as an analogy of how habits work. Water, 'hollows out for itself a channel, which grows broader and deeper; and, after having ceased to flow, it resumes, when it flows again, the path traced by itself before'. So habits, once formed can have a long-standing impact on our well-being. We just have to make sure they are positive ones.

Here are some habits of people who are considered to be successful in life:

- ✪ They read every day and are well-informed.

- ✪ They look after their physical health which, in turn, means their mental health is likely to be good.

- ✪ They get up early in the morning.

- ✪ They are able to switch off and leave their work behind.

- ✪ They are prepared to swim against the tide. Only the dead fish float with it.

- ✪ They are resilient. Not a lot ruffles their feathers.

- ✪ They live each day as if it was their last.

- ✪ They view adversity as an opportunity to learn.

✪ They avoid blaming others and take responsibility for their own actions.

✪ They plan their day the night before.

✪ They take little notice of what others are doing, preferring instead to focus on their own progress.

✪ They are solution-focused.

✪ They are generous and kind, not just to others, but to themselves.

✪ They are clear thinkers.

✪ They are much more likely to innovate than imitate.

✪ They are optimistic.

✪ They are willing to face their fears and sort out problems.

✪ They work from a well thought out set of core values.

✪ They are adaptable.

Take your pick. Don't take on too many new habits at the same time. Be slow and methodical. Allow the establishment of each habit time to bed down and you will soon find you are growing in confidence and health every day.

37

Garden

'Gardening: It's cheaper than therapy and you get tomatoes!'

Staying close to the soil is good for the soul'
– Spencer W. Kimball

Cultivating a garden has been an activity of humankind for millennia. The ancient Egyptians loved their gardens and used them particularly for shade. And if the number of gardening programmes on TV is anything to go by, gardening remains an extremely popular pursuit. The thousands of people who attend the Bloom festival in the Phoenix Park every year is further evidence of that. If you have not discovered the joy of gardening, let me convince you.

If there is too much stress in your life, gardening is one of the best antidotes there is. It removes you from daily stressful routines, it slows you down, you get time to gather your thoughts, it stimulates creativity and you commune with nature. I would challenge anyone to spend an hour in their garden and come out of it not feeling better. If you do not have a garden, you could get an allotment. Alternatively, growing pot plants is an equally popular form of gardening. It is an activity that is available to everyone. No matter what age or ability level, gardening is a most rewarding activity. I continually promote the therapeutic effects of time spent gardening during my talks on controlling stress. Indeed, at the break during one of those talks a very kind lady came up to me and gave me the following poem. I do not know who wrote it (a Google search says it's posted on the greenhouse in the main garden at Ennismore Retreat House in Montenotte), but I am grateful for it all the same:

In Your Garden

In your garden you forget about that unkind thing that someone said -
When you're busy pulling weeds out of the border bed.
You forget the petty things that set your nerves on edge,
When you're turning up the soil or clipping at the hedge.
You forget the unfair way that someone treated you,
When you get out in the garden for an hour or two.
It is strange how quickly you forget your wants and woes,
When you're planting seedlings out or tying up a rose.

You forget the cares that make you feel you're growing old,

When you see the new green shoots come pushing through the mould.

Troubles that seemed big indoors will suddenly seem small,

When you're working in the garden you forget them all.

The list of benefits from gardening is endless. Here are just a few:

◊ There are few better physical activities than gardening. It is reckoned to be as good a physical activity as cycling, walking or running. All muscle groups are worked when we garden. It is both an aerobic (cardio) and anaerobic (muscle) exercise.

◊ It slows us down, bringing us in touch with nature.

◊ It is the perfect escape from too much stress in our lives.

◊ Gardening reduces the chances of getting a whole range of illnesses associated with the sedentary Western lifestyle.

◊ Gardening is for all ages. Indeed, it is the perfect vehicle for different generations to enjoy an activity together. Grandparents and grandchildren can share an activity in which they can equally partake.

◊ Gardening nudges our creative side into action.

◊ It activates our primal instinct of producing food for survival.

◊ Gardening helps us sleep better as a result of its physical exercise and calming influence.

◊ There is a proven reduced risk of developing dementia in those who garden regularly.

◊ Gardening stimulates and nourishes the senses. Perhaps that is why it is so good for our mental health.

◊ Gardening can lift us out of a depression and reduce anxiety. Research has shown a reduced dependence on medication as a result of regular gardening.

◊ It ensures that we have a supply of locally sourced and healthy food. Fresh food from your garden is food at its best.

◊ Gardening can be a tremendously social activity, particularly when we get involved in community projects such as the Tidy Towns or at the local allotment.

◊ The garden can be a great place for meditation. It is the ideal environment to engender a sense of stillness. It is a natural home for meditative practice.

◊ Gardening has been proven to assist in healing those who have been through significant traumatic experiences in their lives.

◊ The garden is a living blank canvas on which any of us can create a magnificent natural masterpiece.

◊ There is no need for special training to create a beautiful garden, even though there are numerous qualifications to be had if a person wants to specialise in a particular aspect.

◊ Gardening can provide a competitive element if a person was to enter their produce in a Horticultural Show.

◊ Gardening is a relatively cheap pursuit.

When it comes to coping with stress, I cannot think of a better activity than gardening to keep it in check. Go and get the gloves on.

38

Join

'I refuse to join any club that would have me as a member.' – Groucho Marx

I was on a tour of Iceland when our guide pointed out a remote village away in the distance. He said that there were only eleven inhabitants and that it was the most isolated village in the world. One of the group commented about how lonely that must be. But the guide quickly responded by pointing out that you can live in the middle of New York City and be more lonely than you would in that tiny enclave on the side of a mountain in Iceland. How right he was. I had that experience when I lived in Los Angeles. I was a student and it was a tough existence trying to make ends meet. The hardest part of it was the lack of company. I had hardly any friends. At my lonely times, I would go down to the sea to watch the sunset and pine for home. That was as good as it got. Then one day I put my name and telephone number down on a contact sheet at the local public tennis courts. It was a way of organising a tennis partner if you had none. It was one of the best things I ever did. The first person to contact me was Diederich. Originally from Brazil, he was the ultimate California dude. He surfed every day and skiied on the weekend. His *joie de vivre* was infectious. We became great friends and played tennis weekly. I ended up sharing an apartment with him for the rest of my time in Los Angeles and we have been firm friends for the last 28 years. He brought me skiing, to nightclubs and a whole range of experiences I would never have undertaken had I not met him. And all from signing up to play tennis in a public park.

Many of us try to cope with stress in ways which may provide temporary relief, but make it worse in the long run. Drinking to excess, overeating, taking drugs and avoiding social situations are just some of the ways people try to cope. It is not uncommon for us to feel that we are the only ones encountering this level of stress and making the choice to remain isolated. The strong suggestion here is that, to avoid the isolation you might be feeling, try something novel and join a group or club.

Joining is one of the best ways to bring our stress levels under control. We meet new people and have new experiences. Having a range of contacts gives us an understanding of how others cope with daily challenges in their lives. You may even meet someone with whom you will form a more lasting friendship. It is no surprise that joining clubs or societies is a big part of university life. It seems that there is recognition within the world of university education of the importance of joining with others towards a common goal at this pivotal time in a young person's life. The same holds true for all of us, regardless of our age, gender or interests. We will reap the benefits of making the effort to join a grouping of some kind or other. Here are just some of the benefits:

◊   You meet new people and may form lifelong friendships.

◊   You may learn a new skill.

◊   Joining is a great way to network.

◊   Joining means you are more likely to commit to a goal and see it through to its conclusion, a very desirable experience in the context of stress.

◊   We are more likely to commit to activities if others depend on our input.

◊   It pushes us out the door when an evening in front of the TV might seem more attractive!

◊   Joining a club boosts our confidence.

◊   Being part of any activity improves our general health.

◊   Joining means we get a break from our usual routine, a necessary means of managing a stressful life.

◊   Joining means having fun, which must be our ultimate objective in life.

There are many activities we can undertake. The first and most important step is to make the effort to pick a new activity to try. Here are some of the options:

Men's Shed

This is a brilliant organisation which has only been on the scene since 2011 but is growing rapidly across the country.

There are 330 Men's Sheds in Ireland at last count. According to the website: 'A Men's Shed is a dedicated, friendly and welcoming meeting place where men come together and undertake a variety of mutually agreed activities.' Men's Sheds are open to all men regardless of age, background or ability. It is a place where you can share your skills and knowledge with others, learn new skills and develop your old ones. Since men are generally considered not to be as good as women at talking about personal issues, Men's Shed is a perfect vehicle to exercise that option if so desired. The quote on the website is 'Men don't talk face to face; they talk shoulder to shoulder'.

Irish Countrywomen's Association

Probably the female equivalent of Men's Shed but it has been around for a lot longer. Their website states: 'The ICA is the largest women's association in Ireland, with more than 10,000 members and over 500 Guilds across the Country. We cook, travel, craft and socialise!'

Toastmasters

'A Toastmasters meeting is a fun and enjoyable learn-by-doing workshop in which participants hone their speaking and leadership skills in a no-pressure atmosphere.' So says their website in what looks like a particularly interesting pursuit open to men and women.

Sports Clubs

The GAA is at the heart of most communities and is one big family of support and recreation. I am unaware of anything like it in any other sport around the world. There are numerous other sports clubs involving both team and individual sports. The health benefits of physical exercise are obvious. But perhaps an even greater benefit is the social aspect.

Evening Classes

The range of evening classes available is mind boggling. There is bound to be at least one class that will pique your interest. Evening classes carry all the benefits of joining a club without any of the long-term commitment. It may just be the option you are looking for.

Gym

Gyms are wonderful places to get started on a self-improvement programme. There is always tremendous help and advice available to set you on the right track. Usually, there are classes available in a variety of different fitness approaches such as aerobics, zumba, spinning, kettle bells or aqua aerobics. Your level of involvement is up to you. Even though the effort to go can be difficult, you always feel better after a trip to the gym.

Bridge

While it is a more sedentary activity, the mind gets a thorough workout after an evening of bridge! It is also a very sociable activity and there are clubs all over Ireland.

Book Clubs

This is a great way to socialise and is becoming increasingly popular. It provides the discipline to read consistently and keeps the mind alert. If there is no book club available in your area, then why not start one? You will find that your local library is a great place to discover any initiatives around reading.

Golf Society

The beauty of a golf society is that you do not have to be a member of a golf club to join. You still get favourable rates at most of the golf clubs visited and society outings are as sociable an occasion as you are likely to find. Golf societies are usually connected to your place of work, a sports club or your local pub.

Special Interest Groups

If you have a particular hobby, you may be surprised to find that there are plenty of others with similar interests. Whether it is computer programming, wine, travel, Lego building, cookery, world war memorabilia or Tiddlywinks, there is bound to be a group with a similar interest. Your task is to find them. The Internet makes that task quite easy. Go find them!

Dating Clubs

I hear mixed reviews about dating clubs. What is clearly evident is that a noisy pub in the middle of your city or town is just about the last place you are going to meet the person of your dreams. And yet it seems to be the option exercised by so many hopefuls. Take the plunge and try something different. You just never know. Some of the happiest couples around have met through a dating agency.

These are just some of the options available to join up with and enhance your life as a result. The message is clear. Being on your own can be stressful. It is very easy to lose perspective when we become more sedentary and isolated. By making the effort to join something new, you just might alter your path in life in a very positive direction. You will never know until you try it. Have a go!

39

Do

'The most effective way to do it is to do it.'
– Amelia Earhart

'I never put off till tomorrow what I can possibly do the day after.' – Oscar Wilde

Procrastination is the avoidance of doing what needs to be done. Whether it is doing more pleasurable things in place of less pleasurable ones, or carrying out less urgent tasks instead of more urgent ones, according to some research, most of us are chronic procrastinators. That means that we engage in this behaviour so often that it interferes with the activities of daily living. Does this sound familiar?: 'I'll wait until Monday to start the diet', 'I'll join the gym in the New Year', 'I'll get a cold if I go walking in that rain', 'The queue is too long'. The reality is that, while we may temporarily relieve the stress of taking action in the short term, the cost of postponement is usually far greater. The eventual outcome and completion of the task is far more stressful than if we had done it at the correct time. Below are my Top Dozen excuses for kicking to touch rather than addressing tasks on time:

1. Technology is probably the greatest distraction of the current age. Being connected means that there is always an excuse to opt out of responsibilities and priorities. This presents a problem, the extent of which has yet to be recognised. Technology is actually making us highly inefficient in the completion of many essential tasks.

2. We put the needs of others ahead of our own. This has to be challenged and rectified. A balance has to be struck between your own priorities and the time you can make available for the needs of others.

3. Avoidance. It is often all too easy to sit in front of the TV when we should be getting on with studies or household jobs. Our minds play tricks and convince us that we need to know how the South Korean economy is doing or which wedding dress a Texas bride is going to pick rather than complete an important report for work the next day.

4. We tend to put things off because of the perceived pain or stress involved. 'I might pull a muscle at the gym' or 'People will be looking at me if I go to the swimming pool' are avoidance strategies.

5. Perfectionism can cause us to hold off even getting started on a job. We can fear the disappointment of not completing the task to our own (usually unreasonable) standard.

This can paralyze us, and the failure to act at all then becomes even more stressful.

6. Habit can be the reason for our procrastination. Have you ever noticed that the same people usually arrive late for meetings while there are others who always arrive on time? When I lived in America, you were considered way out of line if you were even a minute late. Latecomers in Ireland are usually welcomed into the meeting, offered a cup of tea and the next ten minutes is spent briefing them on what they missed in the first half an hour! It is a national trait which I have yet to get used to in the twenty-six years since my return from the US.

7. Lack of confidence can lead to procrastination. If you doubt your capacity to complete a task successfully, the execution of it will be more daunting. This is very common but it is a mindset we must aim to overcome.

8. Fear of failure can cause procrastination. You do not want to expose yourself to negative evaluation by others. It is an irrational fear as the rest of us are usually worrying about ourselves rather than observing you.

9. Fear of success is not uncommon. It is where a person may not want to experience the emotions associated with success because it may bring up emotions related to a past trauma. That past trauma may not be readily known to the person but the two emotional reactions (stress and success) are not dissimilar. Fear of success can be a barrier to taking action for many people.

10. Fatigue. This is a negative spiral into which we can easily fall. We postpone a task because we feel tired, and the lack of action with the accompanying worry about the uncompleted task makes us even more tired!

11. The task is perceived to be too difficult or too great.

12. We are being lazy.

The good news is that we can overcome procrastination by taking some simple steps. As with any initiative to bring about change, the first requirement is to take the step. Make the move. You never know where it might take you.

◊ Identify the cause. Take some time to reflect on why you may be a serial procrastinator. Once you identify what aspect of your make-up is causing the problem, take steps to address it. The list above may help.

◊ Make lists of the tasks you have to undertake. The four categories should be: Work, Home, Social and Personal. List them in order of priority and then be specific about exactly when you are going to complete the task.

◊ Complete the most important tasks first. Morning time is when most of us are at our most efficient. That is when tasks should be undertaken.

◊ Write out a plan for completing the task in hand. If you perceive that the task is particularly onerous, having a clear plan will reduce the daunting nature of it. You will also feel more in control.

◊ Take small steps. We have heard that a journey of a thousand miles starts with one step. A task that is broken down into sufficiently small steps will become much more manageable and you will be far less likely to opt out of it. Remember, being stationary increases the likelihood you will remain stationary. By making a move, you are more likely to stay moving.

◊ Reward yourself for effort. Always build in a reward for accomplishing your objectives. We learned earlier in the book that 90 minutes is the most productive block of time to work on any task. Reward yourself for staying on task for 90 minutes, rather than waiting to complete an entire job.

◊ Have some kind of mantra or saying to remind yourself to stop procrastinating. 'Today is the day', 'Stop thinking, just do it', 'Doing beats stewing', 'Screw it, let's do it' (from Richard Branson) .

◊ Set targets. It is important to have a clear direction so that you have a broad vision of where you want to be when you reach your goals. For example, it might be that you will clear your credit card bill, lose three stone or read five books in a specified time period.

◊ De-clutter. Create an environment conducive to achieving your goals and eliminate any distractions.

◊ Switch off all communication gadgets while you are working on your task. De-clutter your brain.

◊ When you feel like doing nothing, do something, however small. The hardest step is to get started. Put your coat on and get outside the door if you are trying to avoid your walk. Get in your car and drive if you are trying to avoid the gym. Switch off the TV and sit at your desk if you are meant to be working there. You get the picture.

Procrastination raises our stress levels. It creates background noise in our heads and drags us down. It undermines our confidence and makes us feel tired. Turn it around and be that person who gets things done. Deal with issues as they arise and plan meticulously for bigger tasks. You will feel the better for doing so.

40

Express

'The word 'happiness' would lose its mean-
ing if it were not balanced by sadness.'
– Carl Jung

In the days when smoking seemed to be allowed everywhere except downstairs on the bus, there seemed to be an acceptance that the right to smoke outweighed the risk of lung cancer for the rest of us. It was not uncommon for people to light up even downstairs on the bus. If that happened, we would all look away and say nothing. Inside we would be seething but nothing would be said. Thankfully, the smoking ban took care of that problem. But it was a long time coming.

The modern day scourge is how people use mobile phones. How many times have you been in conversation with someone when you suddenly notice they have their head dug into their device reading text messages? You want to say, 'How rude of you, you ignorant prat', but we don't do that. Most of us get mildly distracted and try to keep the conversation going while our absentee conversationalist alternates attention between you and their phone.

It is widely acknowledged that suppressing emotions is not good for our mental health. And conversely, expressing emotions is equally acknowledged as being good for our mental health. Emotions are a form of dialogue between the mind and the body, the heart and the brain. Our emotions support us through the bad times and help us enjoy the good times. They help us to react to difficult circumstances and they influence our decision making. All of us experience frustrations on a daily basis. Rather than suppress our emotions, we need to learn how to express them. How would you typically respond to the following?

◊ You pay a small fortune to attend a concert and discover the band is only playing their 'new stuff'.

◊ When you have waited for fifteen minutes in the supermarket and they open up a new checkout beside you just as you are getting to the top of the queue, and the people who were behind you leave before you.

◊ The referee at your child's Saturday morning match.

◊ Automated answering services that, having brought you through about five different options lists, cut you off for no apparent reason.

◊ You arrive at the supermarket and you don't have a coin for the trolley.

◊ Large lorries driving slowly in the right lane on the motorway.

◊ When you tell your teenager to move their glass in from the edge of the table, they ignore you, and it falls and breaks. Even worse when it happens a second and third time!

◊ You have recorded your favourite TV drama and it cuts off just before the last scene.

◊ You order your steak medium-rare in a restaurant and it arrives cremated.

◊ You put your money in a vending machine and the chocolate bar gets stuck.

The heart is the organ of the body most associated with emotion, whereas the brain is considered the more logical centre. Our aim should be to strike a balance between the two. Logic and emotion are a potent combination. Get it right and we will function well. If this arrangement becomes unbalanced, we become stressed. So should we tear the head off our mobile moron the next time they disrespect us in conversation? Or is there a better way of dealing with the frustrations of life? I believe that we Irish have a difficult time expressing emotions. We bottle it up for fear of causing offence. Men, in particular, are not good at expressing what is going on inside their head. It is probably no coincidence that far more men than women take their own lives – expressing emotion is that important.

Many people seem to believe, albeit subconsciously, that expressing emotions such as sadness is a sign of weakness. On the contrary, it is anything but. Charles Darwin, the great naturalist of the nineteenth century, observed that the emotions serve a fundamental role in the survival of humans. For example, fear sends the message to get away from danger, anger prompts a challenge to a rival, happiness relates to a state that a person would want to repeat.

Daniel Goleman, in his book on the topic, cogently argues that emotional intelligence is probably more important than IQ in predicting how well we function in mainstream society. If we think about it, the people who appear to enjoy that elusive state we call 'success' do so because they appear to be much more in control of their emotions. Rather than academic ability, emotional intelligence has been shown to be a far more relevant characteristic in negotiating life's challenges. Emotionally intelligent people refrain from being obnoxious towards others but have no difficulty acknowledging their own failures or sadness. They are self-aware and have a good handle on their impulses. And emotional intelligence can be learned. Rather than assuming we are born with a particular temperament, research has demonstrated that it is possible to alter brain chemistry and train one's impulses.

Scientists have argued for years about how to classify our emotions. Daniel Goleman concludes that there are probably clusters of emotions, the nuances of which we will probably never fully classify. There are countless different emotions which interact with each other, with varying degrees of intensity. Moods, temperament and even disorder are examples of different levels of intensity of emotion. We should work at acknowledging and expressing them in a way that does not cause offence to others but does not hurt us by remaining suppressed. Here are some of our most common emotions and how to handle them:

◊ **Anger**. Expressing anger is a necessary and normal part of human experience. Some of us choose to bottle it up. Others are more inclined to lash out and regret it afterwards. We have to learn how to express anger in a constructive way. Using 'I' statements, rather than accusing another person, is one such way. For example, 'I am uncomfortable with that' is better than 'you are such an idiot'. The old advice not to allow the sun to go down on your anger is relevant here – when you are angry, express it, but in a constructive way.

◊ **Joy**. This is another emotion that many of us seem reluctant to express, often being more preoccupied with what is not right in our life. By allowing ourselves to experience joy in our lives, we will reduce our stress and produce the happy hormones in our brain that create a very positive cycle of well-being.

◊ **Sadness**. Why do grown men not cry? Perhaps they see it as a sign of weakness. It is not and it is very good for us to cry every once in a while. Feeling sad from time to time does not mean you are depressed. It is a normal human emotion and we should allow it to express itself. If you are stressed, having a good cry will produce oxytocin (known as the cuddle hormone) in the bloodstream. This makes us feel much better and is a great way of regulating our emotions. Interestingly, crying produces similar hormones as laughing – both expressions of emotion are helpful.

◊ **Anxiety**. This emotion illustrates the adaptive nature of the emotions. Too little anxiety and we become lazy and disinterested. Too much anxiety and we become paralyzed. Having the right amount will motivate us. Think about how we are before an exam – a level of anxiety keeps our brains sharp. Like so much of the information about coping with stress, the ideal is to maintain a balance.

◊ **Fear**. This is a self-preservation emotion. It puts us on alert for any dangers which may be around us. While it is wise to take heed of our fears, it is also good to face them. I also like the phrase, 'Feel the fear and do it anyway'.

◊ **Love**. The indefinable. We all know what it is but find it hard to describe it. We need to love and be loved for good mental and emotional health. Love can refer to a love of a whole variety of phenomena such as possessions, pets, country, teams and even other people! So it is a very personal thing. Whatever it is, we need to find our passion in life and express it.

◊ **Guilt**. In Ireland we have this down to a fine art. Maybe we have the Catholic Church to thank for that one – it certainly illustrates the influence of the environment on our emotions. Guilt is something with which we have to wrestle (see the chapter called 'Challenge'). Just as most of what we worry about never happens, most of what we feel guilty about is unwarranted. Challenge it.

◊ **Jealousy**. This is usually born out of insecurity. The economic boom seemed to stimulate this emotion with people constantly comparing – Who has the biggest house? What type of car do you drive? etc. Jealousy is an unhealthy emotion, stimulated by such comparisons. In young people particularly, jealousy is a sign of low self-esteem. The source of jealousy needs to be identified and resolved. Jealousy is an unhealthy emotion.

◊ **Contentment**. This is defined as a state of satisfaction, when the body and mind are at ease. It is probably the ultimate goal for all of us, to reach a state of contentment with our lives. Socrates is quoted thus: 'He who is not contented with what he has, would not be contented with what he would like to have.' When your body and mind are content, take it from me, you have arrived!

Finally, there are some simple things we can do to help us deal with our emotions. They are straightforward so doing them should not be difficult:

✪ **Talk.** So much unnecessary stress emanates from keeping our emotions inside. The best way to alleviate stress is to understand our emotions by talking about them.

✪ **Write.** Describing in writing how we feel will help us to identify our emotion and where it is coming from. Most often, if we can pinpoint the source of the negative emotion, we can find a resolution to the problem.

✪ **Confront.** Emotions left unchecked can be corrosive, even to our physical health. Don't let your emotion become intense to the point that it hurts you. Find the source and tackle it in a planned way.

✪ **Be mindful.** Mindfulness encourages us to recognise emotions, acknowledge them and then let them go. The aim is to keep returning to the present so that toxic emotions are not allowed to interfere with our enjoyment of the present.

✪ **Express.** The chapter title is an important item on your menu of strategies for coping with stress. Expression of emotions, both good and bad, is good for us. This is the dialogue between the brain and the body. We need to listen to our emotions, learn from them and nurture them. So the next time you are watching an episode of *Long Lost Families* on TV, have the box of tissues beside you and let those tears flow!

41

Observe

*'People's minds are changed through
observation and not through argument'*
– Will Rogers

'You can observe a lot by watching'
– Yogi Berra

Have you ever tried to stop for a moment, sit down and watch the world go by? My mother called it 'watching the passing parade'. The longer you linger, the more you begin to notice. By stopping to observe, we develop insights we would otherwise not have had. When I train staff from the caring professions, I place particular emphasis on the skill of observation. Being able to identify the micro-behaviours that signal something is not right is an essential skill for a professional carer. The pallor of a person's skin, the tone of their voice, the pace of their walk – these are all signs that tell you the person is out of sorts. A few minutes of TLC at that point can prevent hours of trying to sort out a major incident later in the day. If we all develop our observation skills there is much to be learned.

You can create a simple observation chart (templates are available online) to help you establish a more accurate picture of what may be going on in your life or in the life of someone you know. Follow the guidelines and you will be amazed at what you will learn.

1. Put the name of the person being observed and the starting date on the form.

2. Identify the behaviour you want to track. This definition is important. It needs to be clear and observable. It can be any behaviour from the use of bad language to hyperventilation. Avoid vague definitions such as 'feeling down' or 'tiredness'. What is the observable behaviour that tells you these symptoms are present? That is your definition.

3. Place an X in the relevant box when the behaviour has occurred. In order to be sure that the data is collected, make sure the chart is available at all times so that each incident is recorded.

4. After a specified period of time, review the data. You may find that the problem behaviour occurs predominantly in the morning, at lunchtime or in the evening. Does it happen more at the weekend? Are there times when the behaviour never happens? If no pattern emerges, could there be a medical

issue? These are all factors which should be considered as you try to understand the source of the problem.

5. Problem-solve a solution (see the chapter called 'Problem-solve') and continue to keep the data to see if your plan is working.

6. Continue to review periodically until you are satisfied the problem has been resolved.

The chart is just a simple tool to enhance your observation skills. It can unlock clues as to why a particular problem behaviour or symptom is occurring. It is equally effective if you are recording your own behaviour or, for example, if you are trying to get a handle on the unruly behaviour of a child.

It is widely acknowledged that most communication is not through words but through body language, so we learn far more from observation than talking. This highlights the importance of sharpening our observation skills. In doing so, we can feel more in control of ourselves and feel more confident in how to respond to others. Either way, it is most helpful to be able to step back and observe:

Observe Yourself

There are times when we only see what we want to see. I can convince myself that the calories won't count if nobody sees me eating the chocolate. But the weighing scales doesn't lie! For example, keeping an accurate food diary will tell you a lot more about why you are not losing weight than relying on anecdotal evidence. If you are feeling particularly stressed, keep an observation chart to determine what is the root cause of the stress. When and where is the stress at its worst? When is there no stress? There is so much information to be gleaned from accurate observation.

Observe Others

It is fascinating to observe children at play. They do so with such freedom and abandon. Children can teach us a lot about how to relax and come into the present moment. Likewise, we can understand much about our peers by observing their body language. Body language can tell us a lot about whether a person is stressed, anxious, depressed or physically ill. Another application of this skill is to observe your role models. What posture do they adopt? What do they wear? How do they engage with people? What makes them appealing to you? By closely observing others, we can learn so much. And remember, the behaviour grid can help unlock the mystery of your child's unusual behaviour patterns if it is kept accurately.

Observe Nature

This is where we slip into the realm of mindfulness. Nature offers us much to soothe an agitated mind. By learning to appreciate nature, we are also teaching ourselves to come into the present, which is where we need to be most of the time. The more we sit and observe, the more there is to appreciate. We live in a beautiful country, so take the time to enjoy it.

Observe Trends

I am old enough to recognise trends that are coming back in vogue not for the first but for a second or third time! Platform shoes are a case in point! Stepping back and noticing the trends that are developing around you creates the opportunity to anticipate problems, rather than having to react to them. For example, letting your children know in advance that they will not be going to Ibiza for two weeks after the Leaving Cert can save a lot of grief later on!

Observe History

It is said that the best predictor of the future is to look at what has happened in the past. There is no doubt that history repeats itself. We can learn much from trying to understand past happenings, including our own previous experiences.

42

Play

'Play is the highest form of research.'
– Albert Einstein

'Work Hard, Play Harder'

Being a competitive tennis player in my younger days, I was keen to pass on the experience to my children. I had also been a tennis coach so it was a dream realised when I first brought them down to the local tennis club to teach them how to play. It started well as we bounced the balls with our rackets. I then showed them the correct grip and stance for hitting the ball. They both told me that I was wrong and ignored my advice! They then started playing chasing around the net and threw their rackets to the side. I lost patience and lapsed into a lecture about how lucky they were to have a tennis court to play on etc. Within five minutes my dream had turned into a mess. The vision of my children holding up the Wimbledon trophy melted away into a game of chasing! And, to cap it all, they were realising what a grumpy oul' fella they had, and were not that keen to play tennis for a while after that. And when they did, they preferred to play with their friends. My children taught me a lot that day. They particularly taught me the meaning of play. It is not about following rules. It is about letting go, having fun and just being in the moment.

Play has been with us throughout history. It is part of every culture in the world. Indeed, much has been learned about the importance of play from the study of animals. Without play we are likely to be at a distinct disadvantage. The leading expert on play, Stuart Brown, has studied prisoners who have committed serious crimes. He found a significant level of play deprivation when these people were growing up. In the absence of play, the brain simply does not develop. The absence of play has also been associated with depression. If we lose our sense of playfulness, we are less able to connect with our world. If you are feeling low, it is necessary to re-connect with your world and play is a good starting point.

Play is a feature of both human and animal development. From the moment we are born we are learning through play. Play is more than just fun – it is how we develop our creativity, how we form bonds and how we solve problems. Play boosts our happiness. Neurologists have been able to demonstrate how the brain develops through play and, for decades now, developmental psychologists have cited the importance of play for children: 'Play allows children to use their creativity while developing their imagination, dexterity, and physical, cognitive, and emotional strength. Play is important to healthy brain development. It is through play that children at a very early age engage and interact in the world around them'.

So why, as we enter our adult years, do we lose the capacity to play? We seem to leave this particular pleasure to our children, but it is essential that we re-engage our capacity for play. Numerous researchers have demonstrated the need and importance of playing. Play stimulates the development of right brain activity, the side responsible for creativity. And it has been shown to enhance productivity. (Employers, take note!)

The eminent psychologist Mihaly Csikszentmihályi coined the term 'flow' to describe completely focused motivation. It is also known as being 'in the zone', a term widely used among sports people. It is a single-minded immersion and represents perhaps the ultimate experience in harnessing the emotions in the service of performing and learning. When we play we are far more likely to enter a state of flow. And, in the context of coping with stress, we are at our happiest when we are in a state of flow.

Play means a lot of different things to different people. It is telling jokes in a restaurant, dancing at a disco, talking to your dog, scoring the winning goal in a final or gazing into your partner's eyes. Play is novel. It is pleasurable. It is creative and it is universal. It can be competitive, but it is probably best when it involves no structure at all. Rough and tumble or simply learning through discovery (think of crab fishing at the beach) is real play in action. Play is a very personal thing. Each one of us has a different take on what playfulness is. The message is to just get out there and play something. Here are some tips:

◊ Have some board games in your home – they are a great way to get all the family involved, or to lift a dinner party.

My favourite board game at the moment is called '30 Seconds' where one person has thirty seconds to elicit the answers to five questions from his team. We have had tremendous, manic fun in our home with it. The choices of board games are endless – make sure you have some at hand.

◊ Play something every day. Electronic games do not count. Football on a field is far superior to football in cyberspace. Avoid getting hooked on electronic gaming as creativity is more often stifled than stimulated.

◊ Join a club (see the chapter called 'Join'). There is great social benefit to pursuing an interest with like-minded people.

◊ Play sports. I am a big fan of sport in all its guises. Playing sport is the ticket through the potentially tough teenage years, both for the teenager and the parents. As soon as they can walk (or even before that!), get your children into sport. They are much more likely to play if you play it also, but it is not essential. And if you have never enjoyed the pleasure, it is never too late to start.

◊ Recall a pleasurable pursuit from your past and try to relive it. What activity gave you most satisfaction? It is very easy to lose touch with previously enjoyed playful activities as responsibilities such as children come along. Rekindle the past and bring some added joy into your world!

◊ Play with children. They have so much to teach us about how to play properly and are not bogged down by rule-bound behaviour. Let them lead the activity and don't take it too seriously; the way life should be.

◊ Be around playful people. Socialise with people with whom you can have a laugh. Live every day like it's your last in the company of people who bring you joy.

◊ Play with puzzles. This is the perfect mindfulness and creative activity. You can shut out the rest of the world when you get stuck into a mind-bending conundrum.

◊ Play an instrument. Music is truly one of life's great gifts, and the ability to play an instrument enhances that pleasure. It opens up all sorts of possibilities. It stimulates our creative capacity and provides a vehicle to meet people in every corner of the world.

Make time to play – today!

43

Imagine

'Imagine all the people living life in peace'
– John Lennon

*'Whether you think you can or you cannot, you
are probably right'* – Henry Ford

You are standing on the first tee of the golf course with your friends. It is a beautiful course and out on the right of the first hole is a lake. You say to yourself, 'Whatever you do, don't hit it in there.'... Do you:

a. Hit your drive down the middle of the fairway.

b. Miss the ball altogether.

c. Curve the ball directly into the middle of the lake.

If you picked 'c' then you are correct. It is extraordinary how we instruct our brains to do the wrong thing by using the term 'Don't'. We do it all the time with ourselves ('Don't make a fool of yourself'), with others ('Don't speak to me like that') and with our children ('Don't pick your nose'). In order to make optimum use of the brain we have to create images of what we want, rather than what we do not want. Continuing the golf analogy, the greatest golfer who ever lived, Jack Nicklaus, has described how he never hit a shot without first visualising it in his mind. Clearly, he did not imagine it going into a lake.

It is estimated that over 60 per cent of us are visual thinkers. Visual thinking utilises the right side of the brain, which is the creative part. Interestingly, most of the greatest geniuses in history were visual thinkers. Bobby Fischer, the famous chess master, Nikola Tesla, the great inventor, Thomas Edison, creator of the light bulb, among other incredible inventions, and Albert Einstein were all visual thinkers. They were able to demonstrate very complex relationships in new and simple ways through pictures. These images could clarify their ideas in ways that went far beyond anything words could illustrate. Indeed, one of the benefits of the digital age is that it assists visual thinkers to demonstrate their ideas without relying on words.

So how does all that help the rest of us? By learning how to visualise our goals and aspirations, we are far more likely to realise them. We have to train our brains to think in a visual, but also positive way. We have to create images of the kind of person we want to be. By visualising what we want both in the short term and in the long term, we are greatly enhancing the chances of its happening. The nervous system does not differentiate between real and imagined events. So when we imagine something, our brain interprets this as if it were happening. Rather than using up our mental energies on negative images, such as thinking what could go wrong ('the plane might crash'), we have to think about a positive image ('I am on my way for a relaxing two weeks in the sun'). This shift in thinking can make a real difference. It promotes the production of 'feel-good' chemicals in the brain thereby reducing our stress levels.

Dr. Paul McKenna outlines a number of visualisation strategies in his series of very accessible books. Guided imagery is one of these whereby another person or a recorded voice guides you through a visualisation process. Outlined below is a very simple visualisation exercise to help create the images, and ultimately the reality, you are striving for:

1. Create a relaxing space for yourself either sitting or lying down. Put on some relaxing background music if you have a preference for it.

2. Close your eyes and focus on your breathing. Breathe slowly in through your nose and out through your mouth causing your stomach to rise up and down.

3. Create a picture in your mind of your ideal place. For example, if it is a mountain scene, notice the colours of the sky and trees. This is nature's canvas at its best. Imagine the smells of wild flowers and pine cones. Feel the grass under your feet and listen to the sounds of the birds. Linger for a while and allow your mind to explore this place.

4. Try to imagine how you would feel after spending time here. Your shoulders will drop, your muscles will relax, your mind will slow down, and there will be no pain in your body from stress.

5. When you are ready, very slowly come back to reality and notice how you are feeling.

6. Repeat this exercise as often as is feasible for you.

There are many variations of this exercise. You can visualise what you will look like as your ideal self. What is your posture? Where are you working as this successful person? What people are in your company? How do you feel? Like anything else, the more you practise visualisation, the better you will be at turning your goals into reality. Being able to use our imagination to enhance our sense of well-being and control is a potent and powerful tool. Most of us do not utilise it nearly enough. We see more and more athletes adopt visualisation strategies to boost performance. All of us can and should do the same.

Remember:

✪ There is no limit to your imagination – all great ideas have emanated from there.

✪ Make sure the images you create for yourself are positive ones.

✪ Visualisation triggers the subconscious. This means that the brain cannot differentiate between a real or imagined memory. If we create positive images in our mind, the brain recalls them as if they were real. As far as the brain and memory are concerned thoughts equal actions.

✪ Since the difference is marginal between what the brain interprets as real and what we imagine, think about how wonderful you are and you will start to feel wonderful.

- ✪ Practise visualisation and you will not believe the results! The more you practise, the better it works. Visualisation can turn a depressed mood into a happy one.

- ✪ Visualisation creates pathways in the brain that will match your vision.

- ✪ Using mental rehearsal is not the preserve of sports people. It is for everyone. Imagine the successful completion of any action before you actually do it.

- ✪ Using the imagination is great fun.

- ✪ Visualisation produces alpha wave brain activity which promotes relaxation and reduces stress. Alpha waves also facilitate clear thinking.

- ✪ Using our imagination increases confidence and boosts self-esteem. Simply put, it makes us happier.

- ✪ Using our imagination stimulates the right half of the brain, the side responsible for creativity.

- ✪ Visualisation aids concentration and clarity. It provides direction which, in turn, keeps us on task.

- ✪ Visualisation is good for the soul. It opens up a world of possibilities. The first step is that we need to be open to utilising our creative potential.

44

Sing

'I don't sing because I am happy. I am happy because I sing.' — William James

Anyone who saw the RTÉ documentary about the High Hopes Choir formed by musical director David Brophy could not fail to have been moved by it. David gathered a group of people who have suffered homelessness and formed them into a cohesive choir which performed in front of a number of different audiences. The transformation in the lives of those who participated was astonishing. Their confidence improved and the unbridled joy of being part of this magnificent project was clearly evident. And perhaps the greatest outcome of the experience for the choir members was the sense of belonging. Friendships were formed, social gatherings were organised and there was a palpable sense among the members of the choir that anything was possible after this experience.

Similarly, there have been a number of different BBC documentaries in which Gareth Malone has formed choirs with a range of diverse groupings. Most often, he was starting from scratch with each of the groups, but the outcome was universally transformative. Happiness pulsed through every choir, and the improvement in self-esteem and confidence among the choir members was palpable. The camaraderie, even through a television screen, was clearly evident. All described it as a life-changing experience. What made these documentaries so moving was that people were drawn from all strands of society. Wealth, status, celebrity or taste meant nothing. Everyone was equal. In some way, participants were exposing the vulnerabilities we all possess and try to keep under wraps. And by taking the plunge, to a person, they came out the other side glowing and feeling on top of the world.

It is probably no coincidence that 32.5 million adults in the USA are members of a choir. The number of children in choirs is probably of the same magnitude. And the numbers are growing. Perhaps they have discovered the fantastic benefits offered by being a member of a choir, which has been described as the perfect tranquilliser. What has been confirmed is that singing produces endorphins and oxytocin, the happy chemicals. Regular singing also reduces the amount of cortisol in the system. Cortisol is produced when we are stressed. It is part of the Fight/Flight/Freeze mechanism described in the chapter 'Understand'. Clearly, singing in a choir is good for our general well-being.

Stacy Hom, a writer for *Time*, described her experience thus: 'Group singing is cheaper than therapy, healthier than drinking, and certainly more fun than working out. It is the one thing in life where feeling better is pretty much guaranteed. Even if you walked into rehearsal exhausted and depressed, by the end of the night you'll walk out high as a kite on endorphins and good will.'

While singing in a choir is not the only way to sing, it does seem to be the one from which people gain most. From a psychological perspective, coming together to enjoy a mutually pleasurable activity as primal as singing has huge benefits. Other forms of communal singing are also beneficial, however. A number of my middle-aged male friends have formed rock groups to sustain them through the menopause and beyond. Outcomes are promising and they haven't fallen out yet!

Whether it is bellowing out opera in the shower, murdering 'I Will Survive' at the local karaoke bar or negotiating your part of Handel's 'Messiah' in front of a packed house in the National Concert Hall, singing is one of the best antidotes to stress there is. I urge anyone who is looking to cope with their stress in an effective way to consider it. Here are just some of the benefits:

◊   Singing is a social activity. It gathers people.

◊   Whether it is in a choir or sitting in a pub, singing creates bonds between people. This applies across different cultures and countries.

◊   Singing improves posture and lung capacity.

◊   If you get involved in singing, you will sleep better.

◊   You will feel better after singing.

◊ Singing improves circulation, lowers blood pressure, and decreases the likelihood of developing heart disease.

◊ Being able to think more clearly is one of the less obvious benefits of singing. This is similar to taking exercise – it clears the head.

◊ Singing enhances our creative capacity. When we are relaxed, we are far more likely to be creative. Singing is a natural relaxant.

◊ Our immune systems are boosted when we sing.

◊ Singing reduces anxiety and depression. This is a scientifically proven fact.

◊ Singing, particularly as part of a choir, boosts our confidence.

◊ Singing, for whatever reason, lifts our spirits.

◊ Singing in a choir is one of the most energising and uplifting activities you can do.

◊ Singing helps us to express emotions. Whether listening or participating, singing forms an integral part of so many of our milestone gatherings. First Holy Communion, weddings, funerals and even singing 'Happy Birthday' at parties helps to express the deeply-felt emotions of the occasion. As we learned in the chapter 'Express', the expression of emotion is a very necessary human experience. Keeping emotions inside can be harmful. Singing helps us to get them out.

◊ Friendships are formed through singing.

◊ Singing is a very healing activity, no matter where you are in your life.

◊ Singing in a group creates a very helpful support network. You can be as supportive to others as they can be for you. Don't forget that.

Finally, I have seen music and singing bring about the most extraordinary transformations in people with special needs. A child who is unable to say their own name will belt out the chorus of a One Direction song effortlessly. Music moves us all. Singing taps into our deepest instincts for healing and survival. It behoves us all to get singing.

45

Relax

'Tension is who you think you should
be. Relaxation is who you are.'
– Chinese Proverb

'Relax. Not every page has to be a masterpiece.'

I have given a number of courses teaching people how to
manage stress. My daughter (from age seven) has reminded
me on a number of occasions that I should be attending that
course and not giving it! It is usually in response to my giving out to her about something trivial like stepping on wires.
Her comment certainly had the effect of grounding me and
reminding me that I need to chill out more often. Indeed, the

longer I work in the field of psychology, which requires me to advise people particularly in times of stress, the more convinced I am of the worth and importance of meditative practice. Every single one of us, from early childhood on, should be engaging in some kind of meditation. It is so good for both our physical and mental health. It helps children perform better at school. From a business perspective, it makes us more efficient and productive. And, in a general sense, it makes us all happier.

As we seem to live in a world which is more and more stressful, the need to put aside time for relaxation is greater than ever. Schools sometimes include one session of mindfulness each week at best. But it needs to be a daily practice. Some of the most progressive companies have relaxation areas for their employees and encourage their use. For the rest of us, while we rarely put our own needs first in the daily humdrum, it is essential that we incorporate some type of relaxation into every day. We are far better able to cope with stress by preventing it than reacting to it. That means developing a routine that we practise every day, even if it is only for ten minutes, although the longer the better. To make the most of your relaxation session, it requires a little planning. Here are some pointers:

Schedule a Time

Early morning is probably the best time to practise relaxation. You may need to go to bed a little earlier to create the time, but it is worth sacrificing half an hour of late night garbage on TV for some quality time in the morning. If morning meditation is not possible, creating time for relaxation is beneficial any time of the day. Planning ahead will ensure that it happens.

Switch Off Technology

It is becoming increasingly evident that being connected means being more stressed. When setting up for a few minutes of relaxation, it is imperative that you are not interrupted by any form of communication device.

Soothe the Senses

If you are having trouble deciding on what type of relaxation ritual would suit you best think about the senses. What type of lighting will relax you? Is there a particular type of music or voice recording you would prefer? What is your favourite aroma? Do you prefer lying down or sitting? When we soothe the senses we are soothing the soul.

Wear Loose Clothing

When we are relaxing we need to avoid feeling constricted. Wear something loose and with which you have a happy association. It may be the colour of the garment or it may have been given to you by a friend. The freer from constraints you feel, the more you will get out of the relaxation time.

Create a Quiet Space

This will make all the difference to how you benefit from the session. If there is a possibility of being distracted, keep looking for a time and place that you will not be interrupted. The whole idea is to create a space for peace and calm. Make sure it is well-ventilated. If it is not possible in your home, a local church might do the trick for some quiet time out for reflection.

Have a Positive Mindset

We don't have to look too far for the negatives. They create tension. Having an 'attitude of gratitude' will put us in the correct frame of mind. Make a determination every time you go to relax that it will be a positive experience.

Develop the Habit

The more we do it, the more we are likely to do it. Particularly at the start, try to set aside time every day for relaxation. It will be the best use of your time all day. Make relaxation a habit.

Slow Breathing Is Best

Whatever type of relaxation method you choose, slow, rhythmic breathing is the cornerstone of relaxation. Faster breathing (also called hyperventilation) is the cause of so many symptoms associated with stress. Get your breathing right and you will be in control of your thoughts.

Avoid Stimulants

Caffeine-based drinks and foods or the other 'old reliables' (nicotine and alcohol) are generally not compatible with the potential benefits of relaxation. To get the most out of your relaxing time, try to cut them out altogether. For some, this is a tall order. Do your best.

You Are Not Alone

When dealing with stressful circumstances, it is very easy to slip into the notion that you are the only one feeling this level of stress. This makes the stress seem even worse. The reality is that we are all feeling stress and we are all looking for ways to alleviate it. Practising daily relaxation exercises is something everyone can do. You should join them. Consider attending a class to set you off on the right footing.

Let Go of Guilt

Dwelling on feelings of guilt is not helpful and impedes relaxation. Let go of them.

Eat Well

Think of the food you put in your mouth as part of your relaxation regime. The more natural it is, the more you will gain from it. Flush out the toxins with plenty of water and nourish your body and soul with good food.

The choice is yours as to which meditative practice you decide upon. Mindfulness, Yoga, Tai Chi, Meditation and Pilates are just some of the possibilities. There are various versions and combinations of these practices. It is well worth trying different ones until you settle on the practice you enjoy best. In the meantime, here are some quick relaxation strategies you can practise almost anywhere:

◊ Play some relaxing music.

◊ Lightly massage your forehead and temples.

◊ Paint a picture.

◊ Say a prayer.

◊ Eat a piece of fruit.

◊ Do a double breath. Two breaths in through the nose and two breaths out through the mouth going' Ha, Ha!' It works.

◊ Place a finger on each shoulder and rotate your arms forward for 20 seconds and backwards for 20 seconds.

◊ Head/neck roll. Touch your chest with your chin. Slowly rotate clockwise for a full circle. Reverse the direction upon completion of each roll.

◊ Give yourself a little treat every day. It does not have to be food and, if it is, make it healthy.

◊ Have a favourite photo where you can see it.

◊   Wrap yourself in a warm blanket.

◊   Stroke your pet.

◊   Soak in a bath with essential oils or bubble bath.

◊   Hum a favourite tune.

◊   Hang wind chimes in your home.

◊   Have the sound of running water near you.

◊   Light a scented candle.

◊   Scent your bed linen with lavender.

◊   Loosen your jaw to relax the rest of your body. Allow your mouth to drop open. It might look odd but it works.

◊   Have a nap during the day.

◊   Look at holiday photos.

◊   Chew gum.

◊   Squeeze a stress ball.

◊   Go for a swim.

◊   Ride a bicycle.

◊   Repeat a positive mantra. 'I am in control' or 'I am fearless'.

◊   Count backwards from 10.

◊   Lie down for a few minutes.

◊   Smell the flowers (literally).

◊   Recall a happy memory.

◊   Avoid all news programmes.

◊   Read a book.

◊   Do a puzzle.

◊   Work on a craft such as sewing or knitting.

◊   Have a good cry every now and then. Let it all out.

◊   Watch a comedy film or go to see a live comedy show.

◊   Delegate responsibilities.

◊   Turn off your mobile phone, particularly when you are walking.

◊   Have a 'Me' day every once in a while.

◊   Give away your cape. You are not a superhero.

◊   Ask for help.

◊   Hug someone.

◊   Splash your face with cold water.

◊   Have dinner by candlelight.

◊   Scream into a towel.

◊   Break tasks into small steps.

46

Move

'Life is like riding a bicycle. To keep your balance you must keep moving.' – Albert Einstein

'When you are going through hell, keep going'

From the time we are born we move. Movement is essential for an infant to thrive and that response continues into childhood. Movement is important for the development of the child on many fronts. It helps the blood circulate. It enables them to explore their world. It develops muscle tone. It ensures their organs are kept working. There are some interesting statistics concerning the movement of toddlers in particular. It is estimated that every day a toddler will move the adult equivalent of 83 rounds of boxing, 30 miles of running, 82 miles of cycling or climbing a mountain twice the size of Ben Nevis, the tallest mountain in the UK. In an experiment in the early twentieth century Jim Thorpe, the foremost athlete in the world at the time, was asked to copy every move of an ordinary toddler. The experiment was to last for four days. After a few hours, Mr. Thorpe had to pull out due to exhaustion. He simply could not keep up with the constant movement of the toddler. This highlights the extent to which movement plays a role in our development.

The question has to be asked, at what point does movement stop? Why don't we keep up this level of movement? Clearly, movement is absolutely essential for our health, and yet, it continues to decline as children progress through school. The points race seems to dominate policy in relation to scheduling. What is the first class to be dropped for an extra-curricular event? You have guessed it. And with the onslaught of video games, children are playing football in cyberspace rather than on a football field. Experts estimate that the lack of movement among the entire population is costing billions of euros as a result of chronic illnesses.

Unfortunately, when we are stressed we get stuck. We find it hard to move in any direction. This can be linked to the third component of the Fight/Flight/Freeze response (See 'Understand'). When we feel under siege, we freeze. Anyone who has had the privilege of travelling through America's national parks will be familiar with the instruction to stay absolutely still if you are confronted with a bear at close quarters. When the bear is gone you are meant to get moving again. However, when we are feeling under pressure in our daily lives, we often find it difficult to move. It seems easier to just curl up in a ball and withdraw. When we are trying to cope with stress, withdrawing is a big mistake. It is imperative that we make ourselves move, to keep the blood flowing, to keep our brains working. We have to stimulate the production of those happy hormones referred to so regularly in this book. When we are stressed, we find it hard to move, but in order to get unstuck, we have to make ourselves move.

By moving I am not just referring to moving the body. I believe that we become overly stressed when our attitudes harden or when our thinking becomes one dimensional. We can slip into a negative mode of thinking and start to believe that everything and everyone is against us. We have to take even minor steps to move out of this negative mode. If not, it can become a habit and a never-ending cycle of misery. There is an alternative. First, we have to get that body moving. Even a short walk to get started or a trip to the gym will make a difference. We have to fight that urge to retreat into our shell when feeling stressed. Second, we must make a determination to shift our thinking into a more positive frame. Adopt an 'Attitude of Gratitude' to influence your thinking. And if possible, move out of your current environment, even if it is only for a short period. It is amazing how a change of scene can promote fresher thinking and a sense of renewal. While the ideal would be a long weekend at a nice spa, realistically, a long walk by the nearest beach or in your local park should suffice. It will undoubtedly enhance your general sense of well-being.

It is interesting that the first thing hospital staff do following just about any type of surgery is to get the patient moving. Clearly, the benefits of movement are recognised, not just for the physical aspects, but also for the psychological gains. If the patient did not move, stagnation would set in and recovery would be compromised. In a general sense, the same holds for all of us. If we allow stress to curtail our activities, we are going to feel even worse and trigger a negative cycle that is difficult to break. There are so many benefits to movement. Here are just a few, each of which applies to our psychological well-being as much as physical:

◊ Movement reduces pain.

◊ We are more likely to avoid injury if we move regularly.

◊ Movement helps to lose or maintain weight.

◊ Regular movement aids digestion.

◊ When we move we boost our immune system and reduce the chances of developing chronic diseases such as heart disease and diabetes.

◊ We sleep much better when we move as our bodies are more likely to have a natural rhythm.

◊ Movement gives us energy. The next time you are tempted to say you are too tired to move (such as going for a walk), remember that moving will give you more energy, not less.

◊ Movement increases flexibility.

◊ Movement enhances our creativity. We are far more likely to come up with creative solutions when engaged in movement such as walking or running than when sitting at home in front of the TV.

Life rarely follows a straight path. We have to be prepared to adapt. The term 'use it or lose it' is apt here. Lack of movement will exacerbate feelings of anxiety and/or depression. So the first thing to do when we feel stressed is to *keep moving*.

47

Laugh

'I told the psychiatrist everyone hates me. He said I was being ridiculous. Everyone hasn't met me yet.' – Rodney Dangerfield

'Laughing is and will always be the best form of therapy.' – Dau Voire

We are told that laughter is the best medicine. This is particularly true when coping with stress. Even at the worst of times, laughter has a role. Have you noticed that after the initial shock of the loss of a loved one, people start to reminisce about the person, which inevitably leads to recalling happier times? It is as if our minds and bodies need to laugh in order to heal. It is a very natural response. There is a whole field of study into the beneficial effects of laughter called gelotology. Laughter is one of the most primal human instincts. Children start to laugh from about four months of age. And they laugh a lot. It is estimated that children laugh between 300 and 400 times a day. Adults are reported to laugh only 10 to 15 times a day. It seems we become more cerebral as we enter the adult years. Children laugh naturally in response to novel situations throughout the day. We adults have to think about it and then decide whether to laugh. By that time it is too late.

Laughter is a universal language. It is recognisable as a response to novel situations the world over, no matter how remote the place or difficult the language. The propensity to laugh appears to be genetic. Studies have shown that some of us are more prone to laughing than others. From a social point of view, it is a very bonding phenomenon. Laughter breaks down barriers and relaxes people. It is beneficial to all ages and groupings. Indeed, studies have shown the benefits of laughter for children, school pupils, business settings, people with special needs, and even prison populations. It is widely accepted that laughter makes us happier, healthier and more energised. It has even been shown to have an anaesthetic benefit in the alleviation of pain. And it is a great way to alleviate tension.

A relatively new phenomenon which is sweeping, not just Ireland, but the world is Laughter Yoga. This is an activity in which the significant benefits of laughter have been recognised and set down into a formal discipline. The interesting thing about Laughter Yoga is that you don't require a quirky sense of humour to participate. The brain does not differentiate between pretending to laugh and actually laughing. A range of exercises is undertaken by participants to promote laughter, whether real or forced. Once you get into the swing of the activity, the laughter becomes more spontaneous. The overriding experience of participants is one of joy and a renewed sense of vitality. Laughter Yoga Ireland has a tremendous website and I would urge anyone to consider Laughter Yoga as an option to tackle stress and even depression.

But if joining a group is not for you, there are many different ways to have a laugh. Meeting friends in a local club or hostelry is the obvious choice. Going to a comedy club or theatre to watch comedy is an excellent way to unwind. Watch a funny movie on TV or in the cinema. Even learning to be able to laugh at ourselves is desirable. If we take life too seriously it becomes dull and stressful. Have reminders around the house to lighten up. Aim to have a household that laughs often and heartily. See the funny side of life. You don't have to be Dara O'Briain to enjoy a good laugh – you just need to be open to the experience.

The benefits of laughing are numerous:

◊ Produces happy chemicals in the bloodstream, which lift the mood and give us renewed energy.

◊ Helps us through difficult times. We often use the term, 'If I didn't laugh, I would cry'. Too true.

◊ Assists learning. We are far more likely to understand and retain information if we have acquired it by having fun and laughter.

◊ Improves teamwork. If an activity is enjoyable, it is going to create greater efficiency.

◊ Brings people together. It creates bonds which make friendships endure.

◊ Increases the flow of blood throughout the body. In doing so, it helps prevent heart disease and other chronic illnesses.

◊ Reduces the production of cortisol and other chemicals associated with stress. There is a sound chemical basis to having a good laugh.

◊ Our breathing becomes more regular when we laugh. If we breathe well, there is a whole range of knock-on benefits. Laughing helps the process of circulating oxygen throughout the body.

◊ Provides both physical and emotional pain relief.

◊ Boosts the immune system.

◊ Having a laugh relaxes the whole body.

◊ Laughing is good for us at a physical, emotional, social and psychological level.

◊ Makes us more resilient, particularly when the stressful and difficult times arrive.

◊ Laughing at situations helps us see them from a different perspective. It helps us to 'think outside the box' thus enhancing our creativity and problem-solving capacity.

◊ Laughter is available to all of us. If it is not readily available, seek out people or experiences which will make you laugh. It is an essential life experience.

We are surrounded with enough negative aspects in our lives that our objective has to be to create a balance. We have to acknowledge the hardships but there is an imperative to

48

Stretch

*'So I said to the gym instructor: "Can you teach
me to do the splits?" He said: "How flexible
are you?" I said: "I can't make Tuesdays."'*
– Tim Vine

'You're only as young as your spine is flexible.'
– Bob Harper

A few years ago I had the privilege of travelling through-out China. One of the most incredible sights was to walk around local parks in the early morning. From the time the sun rises, large groups of people congregate to perform Tai Chi rituals. There were various styles of movement being practised by different congregations. Some of them held sticks with ribbons on the end and moved beautifully in unison. Others followed the more traditional slow Tai Chi movement. Still others practised rituals akin to what we might consider line dancing in the West. Some groups performed to music while others preferred the sounds of nature. It was a marvellous spectacle and as uplifting a scene as I have ever encountered. Every grouping was quite open and inclusive if the various invitations to join in were anything to go by. I witnessed this phenomenon in every city I visited. Interestingly, it was predominantly an older population participating. One young person explained to me that the younger generation did not have much interest in preserving their wellness in this way. But the emphasis on stretching and movement embedded in the Chinese culture left a lasting impression on me.

Stretching is one of the most natural activities, and is something we do from the day we are born. We do it automatically first thing in the morning when we get out of bed along with yawning. Stretching is something we have in common with most animals. If you ever want to observe how to do a good stretch, watch a cat! Women have been noted to be more flexible than men. And while stretching forms a significant part of many yoga routines, its benefits as an activity in its own right are underestimated. Stretching increases muscle strength, enhances flexibility and improves our range of motion. It is a gateway activity into any other athletic pursuits to prevent injury. Most athletes engage in some type of stretching routine before performing. I believe all of us can benefit from stretching before taking on our daily tasks.

The need to engage in stretching has never been greater since the onset of the technological age. People used to work in fields, walk everywhere and go up and down stairs. Now most things are automated. We drive everywhere and there are lifts to take us to every floor. One of the outcomes of these 'developments' is that it has created a build-up of muscle tension. As our sedentary lifestyles have become more established, this tension has increased. Stretching has a role in easing the muscle tension brought on by the age of automation and connectivity.

And while stretching is an excellent activity to help cope with stress, it must be done correctly to avoid injury. It is advisable to seek advice from a trained professional before undertaking a stretching routine. There are numerous excellent stretching lessons available on the Internet if you feel confident enough to go it alone. One of the real benefits of stretching is that, performed correctly, it is never strenuous, which makes it a particularly attractive pursuit for all age ranges and ability levels. If you find yourself bouncing during a stretch or getting to a level where pain is encountered, you have gone too far. And there is no competitive element to the activity. Indeed, the activities I witnessed in the various Chinese parks seemed to create a tremendous sense of camaraderie and belonging. There is no cost to stretching. It can be performed anywhere and at any time of the day. It is a very useful antidote when you are feeling stressed. Five minutes of stretching away from the cauldron can work wonders. Stretching is most beneficial when it forms part of our daily routine, preferably in the morning. As we get older, the benefits of stretching become more evident and necessary to maintain our quality of life. Here are just some of the gains to be made from stretching:

◊   It is a very relaxing activity.

◊   Helps us to maintain our balance and mobility as we age.

◊   Enables us to feel younger. When we move better we feel better

◊ Prepares us for other activities and enhances our performance by bringing about greater flexibility and range of movement.

◊ Gives us energy.

◊ Improves circulation, which has implications in the prevention of a range of chronic illnesses but particularly heart disease.

◊ Reduces and prevents pain.

◊ Done properly, it prevents injuries.

◊ Body awareness is an inevitable outcome of regular stretching.

◊ Allows the body to 'let go' of the stress-inducing thoughts from the mind.

◊ Helps to ensure that we maintain good posture.

◊ Improves coordination.

◊ Helps us to slow down.

◊ A stretching routine can be adapted to suit the individual needs of the person.

◊ Stretching is cheap while also being one of the most effective stress management strategies available to us.

49

Celebrate

*'The more you celebrate and praise your
life, the more there is in life to celebrate.'*
– Oprah Winfrey

*'Life should not only be lived, it should be
celebrated.'* – Osho

A number of years ago I was following Seve Ballesteros
and Colin Montgomerie, two of the world's greatest
golfers at the time, in a practise round at Druid's Glen, a magnificent course in the Wicklow hills. The Irish Open was on.
Part of a large group following the golfers, I heard someone

say 'How'ya Mark?' I turned around and it was Tom Craddock, from my home town of Malahide. We had a chat and I began eulogising this world-class course. As Tom was an outstanding golfer in his day I asked him who had designed it. Turning away in slight embarrassment and in a low voice he said, 'It was me'. It was the most extreme example of Irish modesty I have ever encountered. Tom would never walk on the VIP side of the barrier along with the professionals, preferring instead to be among the crowd. He always made the people he met feel like the celebrity, even though he had been one of Ireland's greatest sportsmen and continued his outstanding career in golf course design. Tom is the most iconic and uncelebrated figure ever to come from Malahide. Sadly, Tom passed away a few years later before ever being truly recognised for the brilliant and generous role model he was. That moment with Tom in Druid's Glen taught me the importance of acknowledging our accomplishments. We should be generous enough to celebrate the achievements of others, but we should also be proud to celebrate our own.

Is this another one of our Irish quirks, the reluctance or inability to acknowledge a job well done? There seems to be a fear of being viewed as boastful, and indeed we often seem to resent those who enjoy success. Well that has to change. There is nothing wrong with acknowledging and lauding a job well done or an important milestone. We also need to include the small accomplishments as well. Your child's first picture of a house, tackling a problem successfully, even waking up in the morning should all be celebrated. We spend far too much time dwelling on the negative aspects of our lives. Celebrating the good stuff will take us out of that frame and compels us to focus on the positive side of life. A celebration is a public acknowledgement of a person or an achievement by means of a social gathering or enjoyable activity. Whether it is at home or in the work setting, we need to celebrate regularly.

At the start of the season following Leicester City's extraordinary victory in the Premier League soccer competition, Claudio Ranieri urged his players to forget the previous season and focus on the new one. I would take issue with his approach. Winning is a habit and celebrating winning is an acknowledgement of that. If we forget about our past achievements we are not going to build on them. I believe Mr. Ranieri should encourage his players to strut like the wonderful champions they are. Then they would be more likely to win again.

Celebration means bringing people together. Acknowledging achievements motivates us to do more. Many of us might say that we do not like to be the focus of attention but we dislike being ignored even more. It is a fundamental principle of behaviour that we are far more likely to repeat a behaviour for which we have been recognised. Sadly, most workplaces have yet to recognise this phenomenon. When was the last time your efforts were acknowledged in your workplace? We could ask the same question about many households. And yet, being celebrated gives us confidence and builds our self-esteem. It motivates us and makes us more productive. Children love a celebration, however small. Adults should too. If nothing else, celebrations bring us together either as a work grouping, a team or as a family. Absence of celebration diminishes the value of achievements. Celebrations light up the mundane. They create happiness. They are an essential part of living a good life. They need to be a regular part of all our lives.

Remember:

✪ Celebration alleviates stress.

✪ Recognising something done well shifts the focus away from problems. Life is not all about problems. We need to be reminded of that from time to time.

✪ A celebration, however small, brings people together.

✪ Celebrations create a sense of connectedness with traditions from the past. There is a reassurance that goes with such reminiscence.

✪ Celebration is a means of showing our appreciation of those we admire!

✪ There is a natural human pleasure which comes from celebrating.

✪ Celebration can light up an otherwise dull day.

✪ Celebrating successes, however small, builds our confidence.

✪ By celebrating milestones, we are telling the person that they are important in our lives. (Although this seemed to get a little out of hand in America where they used to have Secretaries' Day, Love Your Pet Day, Janitor Appreciation Day among others, when people would feel forced into buying cards and gifts for random groupings!)

✪ Celebrations bring out our creative and playful sides.

✪ Having a celebration brings about rejuvenation and renewal.

✪ Having celebrations can strengthen family bonds.

As the song goes, 'Celebrate Good Times' – it shifts our focus from more trying or mundane times, and reminds us to be glad we are alive. Celebrations give us a sense of belonging. We need to celebrate at every opportunity.

50

Invest

'The best investment you will ever make is in yourself.' – Warren Buffett

I f you have made it as far as reading this chapter then, *well done*! That is a good first step towards investing in yourself. You will probably have gathered that this chapter has nothing to do with investing money. It is all about investing time and resources into you so that you can be at your absolute best. I am struck by the fact that the most successful investor of all time, Warren Buffett, recognises the value of investing in ourselves. He views it as a sound long-term investment. While funds and financial portfolios fluctuate, investing wisely in ourselves adds permanent value. For example, if you have completed a course in mindfulness, even if you are not using it all the time, you can always come back to it at a later date.

I believe that we should do something for ourselves every day. Whether it is making time to exercise, attending a class or meeting up with friends, it is imperative that we take time for ourselves on a daily basis. Without wishing to get too sloppy about it, if we do not love ourselves, it is less likely others will. Some estimate that we should spend 3 per cent of our total income on self improvement – all the evidence points to a huge return on this type of investment. If you are a parent, the likelihood is that you are the last person on whom you will spend any disposable income. And yet this is a false economy. If you are not operating at your best, you will not be able to be the parent you aspire to be. In order to be at your best, you have to create time and space for yourself. Once again, it all comes down to establishing a balance in which all needs are catered for, including your own.

So the first task is to make the time to pursue your own needs and interests. Part of that is to identify exactly what they are. Make sure that whatever you decide to do for yourself is enjoyable. Abandon activities that you do not find enriching. Try something different if you are feeling adventurous. Rekindle old friendships or join a new group if there are no friends available. Shift your frame of reference from putting the needs of others first to prioritising your own. This can be done with a degree of subtlety but certainty nonetheless. Make your own health your main priority. By doing this you will benefit those around you. There is no time like the present. Start now! Here are some ideas to get you going:

Make a List

A very positive step is to take the time and put together a list of 100 things you would like to accomplish. (Some people call this a bucket list.) Even if you never complete all of them, you will have a good time putting the list together. Give each entry some thought. Allow your imagination to flow freely. Even if the prospect of achieving your goals may seem unrealistic at this time, you never know what surprises life can send your way. Without the aspiration, there is no chance of its happening. When you submit the wish to paper, it immediately has a focus and a direction.

Hire a Coach/Trainer

Whether it is to increase physical fitness or learning how to sing, starting out on the right track is critical. You will make more progress more quickly with a person to mentor you. They will keep you motivated and accountable. They will know how to develop correctly and when to stop. A trainer can provide objectivity that is simply not available when you go it alone.

Attend Workshops/Seminars

These can be one-day events or courses that run over an extended period of time. Not only are you likely to acquire new information, these events are very sociable affairs which enhances the learning experience even further.

Take Time Out

Have a 'me' day every once in a while. This does not have to be a particularly strenuous day. If you decide to stay in bed until lunchtime, then that is fine. The whole idea is to do as little as you can so that you can resume normal service refreshed and re-vitalised. Make sure to do this at least four times a year.

Pamper Yourself

The obvious version of this is to spend a day having spa treatments. While this may be considered an extravagance by some, it is at the core of why we have to make our own needs our top priority. Book some spa treatments because you are worth it. We have no problem spending money on television packages or overseas holidays. Ease back on those extravagances and keep the pampering.

Socialise

Make a point of nurturing friendships. Invite people to your home for an evening of banter and chat. Join friends if you have them (many of us don't) in the local hostelry, and find way to make friends if you don't. Recognise the importance of social contacts. There are no set rules. Step out of the comfort zone, and make the effort to get to know new people.

Buy a Quality Item of Clothing

Even if you have to save up for it, demonstrate your worth to yourself by buying yourself something. A quality garment will boost your confidence and make you feel good. Do this at least once a year.

Read

Gaining knowledge is a great way to build confidence and self-esteem. Reading for half an hour every day will create more than just a knowledge base. It will relax you while at the same time expanding your learning.

Do Something You Have Never Done Before

This is what makes life interesting. You will not regret exploring a new interest. Novelty is what motivates us and keeps us on our toes. For example, if you don't like to cook, take a cookery course. Great champions turn their weaknesses into strengths. Let that be your starting point in picking a new pursuit.

Have Fun

If there is not enough joy in your life at the moment, go out and find some, even if it means joining a joke-telling class! We get one chance. Make the most of it. Live every day like it is your last.

Maintain a Good Work/Life Balance

Keep reminding yourself that we are all dispensable. Our time away from work is every bit as important as being there. Continue to monitor whether you are spending too much time at work and not enough time investing in yourself or your family.

Make Time for Family

Regardless of how distant they may be, family are the people most likely to be there for you in both good and bad times in life. Nourish those relationships.

Finally, I will conclude this final chapter with the words of my esteemed colleague, Dr. Jim White, creator of the internationally acclaimed Stress Control programme:

Believe in Yourself!